THE
ORVIS®
GUIDE TO MUSKIES
ON THE FLY

KIP VIETH

LYONS
PRESS

Guilford, Connecticut

An imprint of The Rowman & Littlefield Publishing Group, Inc.
4501 Forbes Blvd., Ste. 200
Lanham, MD 20706
www.rowman.com

Distributed by NATIONAL BOOK NETWORK

British Library Cataloguing in Publication Information available

Library of Congress Cataloging-in-Publication Data

Names: Vieth, Kip, 1964- author.
Title: The Orvis guide to muskies on the fly / Kip Vieth.
Other titles: Guide to muskies on the fly
Description: Guilford, Connecticut : Lyons Press, 2020. | Includes index. | Summary: "The essential Orvis primer on fly-fishing for Muskies, addressing every requirement of the sport and providing an excellent foundation for years of pleasurable fishing"-- Provided by publisher.
Identifiers: LCCN 2019059389 (print) | LCCN 2019059390 (ebook) | ISBN 9781493040001 (paperback) | ISBN 9781493040018 (epub)
Subjects: LCSH: Muskellunge fishing.
Classification: LCC SH691.M8 V54 2020 (print) | LCC SH691.M8 (ebook) | DDC 799.17/59--dc23
LC record available at https://lccn.loc.gov/2019059389
LC ebook record available at https://lccn.loc.gov/2019059390

♾™ The paper used in this publication meets the minimum requirements of American National Standard for Information Sciences—Permanence of Paper for Printed Library Materials, ANSI/NISO Z39.48-1992.

You always hear faith, family, and friends. Without my faith, family, or friends, I couldn't have pursued my dreams and have the business that I have today. I thank God for all the blessings that I have received. My faith has kept me grounded and looking at the bigger picture. I dedicate this book to my family for letting me follow this crazy journey that I've taken them on. My wife Linnea, daughter Grace, and son Truman have sacrificed a great deal to allow their husband and father to chase his passion. A guide is only as good as his supporting cast. I have the world's greatest. Boat washers, lunch runners, secretary, editor, and counselors—they have done it all. I just row the boat. They do the rest. I love you and appreciate all you have sacrificed for me.

Many of the photos that grace the pages of this book are from my dear friend Jon Luke. His spirit and passion for fly fishing were amazing. He was the other founding father of our annual muskie camp each October in northern Minnesota. We spent many hours sitting around a campfire solving all the world's problems and trying to find the world's best muskie bourbon. We shared so many memories. Muskie camp is not the same without him. He kept me grounded and looking at the big picture. He was always there for some sage advice in the crazy world of the fly-fishing industry. My hope is that this book is good enough to celebrate one hell of a fly angler and an even better human being.

◆CONTENTS◆

►◆ACKNOWLEDGMENTS◆◄

The Orvis Company has been a huge part of my success. They had faith in me to support and help grow Wildwood Float Trips to where it is today. The entire crew at Orvis has been nothing short of amazing. From the CEO to the managers at the stores throughout the country, I have felt the support from everyone. A special thank-you to Scott McEnaney, Peter Kutzer, Tom Rosenbauer, and Bill McLaughlin—four gentlemen that have really been behind me and have encouraged me from the very beginning of my relationship with one of the finest companies in the fly-fishing industry. The fact that they let me host the Orvis Muskie School is still amazing to me.

To my mother and father I owe a great deal. They let me sit on my rock and fish for hours on end at the Wildwood Retreat. That spot still holds a special place in my heart and might be one of my favorite spots in the world. Though my father still thinks I don't have a real job, he did take me on many fishing trips and showed me the wonders of fishing.

I want to thank a few of the guides and friends that were kind enough to take me under their wing and expose me to these wonderful creatures. These folks are some of the best muskie guides and anglers in the world, and I am forever grateful for their generosity in the very tight-lipped world of muskie anglers.

I'd like to thank all the guides and fellow anglers that contributed to this book, including Bob White, Russ Grontarek, Matt Miles, Bill Sherer, Greg Pearson, James Johnsey, Eric Grajewski, Andy Pappas, and John Anderson. I appreciate these folks taking time to help me with the book and offering their expertise and wisdom so that we all can get a better understanding of muskies.

I wouldn't have gotten into this game without the following people who helped me and encouraged me along the way: Troy Andersen, who guided me to my first muskie on the fly a lot of years ago. Gabe Schubert, aka Muskie Jesus (don't call him that to his face—he hates it and will never forgive me for giving him that nickname), who probably ties the most beautiful and effective muskie flies in the world and is simply a muskie savant. Russ Grontarek, Gabe's partner in crime and all-around fishy cat. Russ was also kind enough to supply some brilliant artwork for the book. Brad Bohen, who is probably more responsible for bringing the muskie-on-the-fly game to the mainstream than anyone I'm aware of. He is a shameless promoter of the sport, and for that I will always be grateful. Rising waters lift all drift boats. Bob White, friend and world-renowned sporting artist, who is always there with encouragement and advice. Pat Ehlers, shop owner, who had the faith in me and our fisheries to host muskie trips with us.

Travis Frank has always helped when I had a muskie question and has made me a better angler. He taught me valuable lessons about muskies and ways to approach them. Tim Landwehr is always there with encouragement and advice. He runs one of the greatest guiding operations in the Midwest, and his entire crew is special. I'm still waiting for that invite, though. Bob Bickford and John Edstrom, two of the best smallmouth guides in the country, welcomed me into the fold when I first started. They both have been good friends and allies for the resource here in the Upper Midwest. The guides that work for Wildwood Float Trips—Nick, Josh, Gabe, Russ, and Bobby C—are some of the best dudes to share a river with. Thanks for all you guys do!

I would also like to give credit to all the natural resource professionals throughout North America who work tirelessly on behalf of all the muskie anglers out there. They're the unsung heroes. Their research helps us all better understand muskies and what makes them tick. They are really doing some groundbreaking research. I particularly want to thank Chris Kavanaugh, a fisheries biologist here in Minnesota, who was kind enough to answer any questions I had about muskies and their management. He is a great resource and advocate for our fisheries.

Most of all, I want to thank all of my clients who have blessed me with their business so I can do what I love to do. I have learned more from clients than any other source, and without them there is no Wildwood Float Trips. I am blessed beyond measure and am thankful every day I get to do what I do. I hope you enjoy the book.

◆ INTRODUCTION ◆

I have never caught a muskie on a fly rod. I have never even had a muskie follow a fly although I have made a few casts in waters where I know muskies exist. I have never caught a muskie on conventional tackle. I have seen a couple in the water. So why am I writing a foreword to a book on muskie fishing? Because if I ever want to get serious about muskie fishing (which I do when I grow up), I want Kip next to me in the boat, and having this book is the next best thing.

But I do know a few things about putting together a how-to book on fly fishing. I grew up learning to fly-fish through books, before the internet and video days, and in the past fifty-five years I've read most of them. And I have also written a number of them. I know what a struggle it is to describe an entire fishery and to attempt to incorporate everything I know, plus many things other fly fishers have taught me, into a few scores of thousands of words. Plus finding the right photographs and diagrams to illustrate the point. And contacting experts in the field to share their knowledge and to keep me on track.

Kip has included everything I would possibly want as a novice, or as an experienced muskie angler looking to expand their knowledge. Natural history. Habitat. Seasonal factors. Best places. Tackle. Flies. Casting. Retrieves. Ways to get these reportedly infuriating monsters to actually commit and take a fly. Playing, landing, and releasing them. And what I especially like about Kip's approach is that he does not try to answer it all himself, but gives credit where it's due. He interviews biologists, rod designers, and casting experts.

Kip is a great writer. He is an expert storyteller and his explanations are clear and concise, tempered with common sense and humor. He doesn't take himself too seriously, which is like a fresh breeze in the fly-fishing world of experts. He also includes a couple of ideas that I'm going to steal in my next book. One is a summation at the end of every chapter, entitled "Kip Notes," where he emphasizes the high points of each chapter. Another is an especially useful section at the end called "A Different View," where he interviews or shares an essay from another muskie expert from a different part of the country. Too often fly-fishing authors are regionally focused and expect that the suggestions in their book will apply to fisheries around the country. That is not always the case, and can lead some readers down the wrong path, or at least send them on a detour that must be corrected later. A really helpful touch that shows the research and work that went into Kip's book.

To sum it up, as an aspiring muskie angler I think this is the perfect book. I encouraged Kip to write it, and I'm very proud of being a small part of what will be the definitive guide to muskie fishing with a fly rod for many years to come.

—Tom Rosenbauer

CHAPTER ONE

MUSKIE: THE FRESHWATER FISH OF MYTH AND LEGEND

To a warmwater angler, no fish has more lore, history, or legend surrounding it than the muskie. Countless stories about these mysterious creatures have been written and told for hundreds of years. You can't pick up a magazine, turn on a fishing show, or look at social media without seeing references to muskies and the anglers and guides that pursue them.

It is hard to say this, but muskie fly fishing has become almost mainstream. If you told me twenty years ago that muskie fly fishing would grow to the point where it is now, I would have called you crazy. As I was researching this book, I looked at all kinds of other books and studies on the subject of muskies. Most of them were slanted toward the conventional gear angler. Tales of guides, strategies, record books, biological studies—you name it, I bet I probably looked at it.

One thing that really struck me was a chapter on fly fishing for muskies in *The Complete Guide to Musky Hunting* by Jim Saric and Steve Heiting. Both are well-respected muskie hunters and have worked for *Musky Hunter* magazine and TV show. The book was written back in 1999, when fly fishing was just beginning to gain acceptance as an effective way to pursue muskies. To be honest, if you fly-fished for muskies back then, most people thought you were a couple cards short of a full deck. The fly-fishing chapter in Saric and Heiting's book was a total of five pages long, and two of the pages were pictures. Now, more than twenty years later, there are several books devoted exclusively to fly fishing for muskies, including this one. To be fair to the gang at *Musky Hunter*, the fact that they included a section on fly fishing in 1999 was impressive. They saw value in it and that in certain situations it could be an effective way to pursue muskies. They have always been on the cutting edge of the sport and supportive of all muskie anglers.

There were a few guides working in northern Wisconsin at the time, but not many. Bill Sherer was one of the very first that I know of, having opened a fly shop back in 1994 in Boulder Junction. He led the charge, so to speak, and put muskie on the fly on the radar here in the Upper Midwest. He's still at it and still one of the most knowledgeable guides out there.

The paradigm shifted completely in 2011 with the release of the movie *Musky Country: Zero 2 Hero*. Filmmaker Robert Thompson tagged along with my friend Brad Bohen and his merry band of brothers in northern Wisconsin. The film did a great job of showing what muskie fishing on the fly was all about. The fact that Brad caught a world record at the time on film didn't hurt either. The film was placed in the Fly Fishing Film Tour in 2011 and was named DVD of the Year by the IFTD. Thousands of fly anglers got to see what a bunch of dedicated muskie-on-the-fly nut jobs do here in the Upper Midwest. It brought muskie fishing into the light. It was no longer just a thing that a bunch of jack pine savages did in the Upper Midwest. Like the movie *A River Runs Through It*, which caused rapid growth in the fly-fishing industry, *Zero 2 Hero* gave a big boost to muskie fly angling. Anglers saw that it was real and could be done. Muskie on the fly never looked back, and it has cemented itself into the fly-fishing culture.

Fly fishing for muskies is here to stay and is only going to get bigger and better. Conservationists, fisheries biologists, manufacturers of fishing gear, and anglers all over the world have been bitten by the muskie bug. It's not hard to see why. The rich history and lore of the fish can't help but draw one into this crazy sport. The muskie is in many ways like a mythical creature that swims, always lurking and remaining mysterious to its pursuers.

The Wildwood Retreat circa 1940s. In the background is the rock that I spent countless hours of my youth fishing.
KIP VIETH

Growing up in Wisconsin, the muskie was king. My great-grandmother owned and ran a resort in the Northwoods. Here, in northern Wisconsin, the muskie is looked at as some sort of god. It is revered as much as a fine five-year-old piece of aged cheddar cheese. Muskies are held to a different standard than any other warmwater fish, and after you have chased them for a while, you'll begin to understand why. When your home state has a muskie statue that measures four and a half stories tall and has over 50,000 visitors a year, you know that we are serious about muskies. Presidents, sports figures, and celebrities have traveled from all over the world to chase them. They are among the most sought-after gamefish that swim in freshwater.

As a youth I was immersed in tales and lore of fish the size of a log and with teeth like razors. All one has to do is to look at the mouth of a muskie and realize that they are all business. They're the king of freshwater, and you can't help but be drawn into the legend of these fish. Perhaps no fish has as many stories written about it, and none sum up the lore of the fish like those surrounding the world record muskie. People are still writing about it to this day, and it happened back in 1949. The legend and lore of Louie Spray and Cal Johnson, and who really caught the world record muskie, is still a hot debate in certain circles.

Louie was a life-loving Northwoods man and was known as a fellow that liked to live on the edge, and this sometimes included scrapes with the law. His 69-pound-11-ounce fish is recognized by the Freshwater Fishing Hall of Fame in Hayward, Wisconsin, as its world record. The International Game Fish Association (IGFA) doesn't recognize Louie's fish as the world record, however—it recognizes Cal Johnson's fish that weighed 67½ pounds. The reason it doesn't recognize Louie's fish is that it had two bullet holes in its head. This was common practice back then. Guides would often carry a pistol or rifle to shoot these monsters in the head. There was no catch-and-release back then, so they would shoot them to make landing them easier. It was perfectly legal in 1949, when both fish were caught. Louie's mount was lost in a fire, adding more mystery and intrigue to an already controversial story. There are also rumors that Louie bought his fish for $50 from noted Chicago Mafia member Joey "Doves" Aiuppa. Some people also say that Louie stuffed lead in the fish, that it wasn't weighed properly, etc., etc. If this had taken place in today's world of social media, one can only imagine the storm that would be brewing.

You can still see Cal's fish displayed in Hayward. I remember walking into the famous Moccasin Bar with my family as a young boy to see it. Not much has changed at the Moccasin almost forty years later. When you walk into the bar, it's like stepping back in time. It is a true Northwoods bar in the heart of Hayward, harkening back to the days when Louie and Cal and many other old-time muskie wranglers walked the streets there. As you can imagine, no other fish that swims in freshwater is celebrated like that of the muskie, especially in the Upper Midwest. The muskie is king in the Upper Midwest, and the Upper Midwest is the epicenter of muskie fishing. The rich history only adds to the mythic legend that the muskie has become. It is and always will be a big part of the culture of fishing here in the Upper Midwest.

The real celebrities, however, are the everyday anglers who have a passion and zeal for the magnificent creatures. A perfect illustration of this is one of my childhood friends' grandmother. My friend and his family loved to chase muskies. They loved all outdoor activities, but the muskie held a special spot in this family's DNA. Now, my family also loved to fish, but was never bitten by the muskie bug. We were your standard Upper Midwest walleye chasers. Walleye fishing never took a firm grip on me, however, and I was always looking for different fish and ways to fish. My friend's family was the first to introduce me to trout fishing and the wonders of the Driftless Area. Exploring the trout streams of the Driftless Area with worms and an ultralight spinning rod was simply heaven on earth to me. I loved the intimacy of a trout stream and everything that came with it. I would eventually see someone fly fishing, and the die was cast. Fly fishing consumed me, and with the help of this family, I would eventually discover my addiction to it. I was known in my family as the kid that fished. It didn't matter what, where, or when, I just loved to fish, period.

My friend's family was perhaps the first family that I knew for whom muskies were a way of life. They studied them and approached them differently than any other fish. It was my first exposure to putting science behind one's fishing. It opened my eyes to putting together a game plan when I approached my fishing. It was a very valuable lesson at a very young age. Trout fishing for them was just a filler until muskie season started. When I would go down to my buddy's house to hang out, there was muskie gear all over the place. Muskie rods were hung neatly in the garage and basement, and loads of lures were stored and ready to go at a moment's notice. In the basement were trophy muskies that were mounted as evidence of battles won. All of this only added to my fascination with them. My friend's family would plan their vacations around muskies. They would spend most, if not all, of the month of August in northern Wisconsin on their favorite lake, Lake Tomahawk. They owned a cabin on the lake for the sole purpose of chasing muskies.

The head of the family was my buddy's grandmother. She was already getting up there in age when I was introduced to her. She loved to cast for muskies as much as any member of the family. Now, she was ahead of the curve as far as female anglers were concerned. A lot of other anglers we knew found it amazing that Grandma could fish just as hard as anyone. I never thought it was that big of a deal, knowing of my own great-grandma's outdoor exploits. She was another woman way ahead of her time. She and her husband started their resort in the 1930s. In 1942 my great-grand-father died at the age of 51, leaving his 46-year-old widow and four daughters to run the Wildwood Retreat Resort at a time when women just didn't do things like that. My great-grandmother ran the resort by herself with the help of her kids and grand-kids into her 80s. To say she was a strong woman would be a bit of an understatement. She planted an outdoor seed in our family that continues to grow and flourish.

Spending a lot of time outdoors was part of my friend's and our families' life-styles, and these grandmothers had a lot to do with that. Families like these aren't as common as they once were, but we're still out there. Families and passionate anglers that love muskies are the folks that will keep the lore and the legend of the muskie alive. They are the main reason that the outdoor culture exists throughout this great county. I thank wonderful role models like my great-grandmother, my buddy's family, and my own family for showing me the great wonders of our natural resources and the sheer pleasure of spending a day in the out of doors.

I would listen to these stories by the resort's guests and guides with eyes the size of saucers, wondering how such a beast could swim in such a beautiful place. I would often think of them as I swam in the lake that the resort was on. I often wondered if one of these beasts might be lurking below me as I swam out to the raft that my cous-ins and I would play on. So, the addiction was planted at a very early age. It was part of life in the Northwoods, and it was impossible to escape for a young boy that loved everything that swam, flew, and crawled in my sanctuary of the Wildwood Retreat Resort. The passion was fueled by the great people that drifted in and out of my life as a youngster. Fast-forward fifteen years, and it has become the cause of sleepless nights,

The fish of 10,000 casts?
AARON OTTO

sore muscles, and more frustration than most anglers will ever experience. Throw in the fact that I'm a fly angler, and you have taken a difficult proposition at best and just doubled if not tripled the difficulty to be successful.

Folklore says that the muskie is the fish of 10,000 casts. A lot of this is hype by novices and the media. Is it difficult? Yes. But it doesn't need to be that tough. Using your head and connecting a few dots can cut the curve in half. The pursuit of muskie on the fly is not for the faint of heart. It requires dedication, smarts, and most of all, mental toughness. Muskies are the apex predator in freshwater. Just consider them the great white sharks of freshwater. They are afraid of virtually nothing. I've had them swipe at my oar in the water. If the idea of something that mean and mysterious swimming in a freshwater lake or river doesn't get your blood pumping, I don't know what will. When their trigger flips and they want to eat, they'll consume almost anything they can get down their throat. Ducklings, birds, frogs, pike, and other fatty fish are all fair game when it's time for them to eat. The trick is figuring out *when* they want to eat. This is the age-old question that continues to haunt muskie anglers, and probably will till the end of time. How can a fish that will eat almost anything when they're hungry be that temperamental? When you figure that out, let me know.

With all that being said, why would anyone want to pursue such an elusive fish? It's not often that we measure success by the number of fish we see follow our fly. Many times, I'll be sitting by the fire with buddies after a day of fishing and catch myself saying we had a great day because we had seven follows. Can you imagine going trout fishing and saying we had a wonderful day because we saw four trout rise? They're elusive and mysterious, and they're muskies after all. A big muskie is a trophy like no other in freshwater fishing. Catching a big muskie on a fly is perhaps the hardest thing an angler can do. I know there are many saltwater anglers out there that may argue my point, but let's look at it a bit closer.

Muskies are perhaps the most unforgiving fish that swim. They don't care how old you are, how long you have been fishing, what sex you are, where you're from, or who you are. They are the great equalizer. One of my friends said to me, "No one is that special." He is right. I don't care how many books you've written, Instagram followers you have, or awards or tournaments you have won, or how much money you have or number of fish you boated this season—no one is special in this game because the pendulum swings both ways. If you don't know humility now, you will as a muskie angler. No one, and I mean no one, is as good as they think they are, and no one is as bad as they feel after they blow a big fish.

First off, you're casting a fly the size of a small animal all day to a fish you can't see. This may go on for three days before you get your first contact, let alone an eat. The mental game that is required to be successful is daunting. This mysterious fish only eats when it wants to eat. They may follow, tease, and tempt the angler into some sort of false hope, only to have that hope dashed by their fickle ways and habits. I mostly fish in the fall and early winter. This means frozen hands, feet, and guides to make it just that much more difficult. The fish seem to know this and seem to be a little more active on the crummiest of days. Cold rain, snow, and wind chills in the single digits are all part of the game in the Northwoods of the Upper Midwest. Muskies' mouths are made of iron, so you may have them eat, but if your strip-strike is bad (remember those cold hands), the fish doesn't play nice, or if you lift the rod like it was a 13-inch brown trout, you lose. All the work and frustration of hours casting to a unicorn, and it simply doesn't go the way you have played it in your head repeatedly. The moment the fish eats your fly, you often lose all semblance of reality. Things just have a way of blowing up when that moment comes. I always tell my clients that they're most likely going to blow their first muskie eat, so get used to it. There is no way to prepare a fly angler for seeing a freshwater fish that big eat your fly. I can tell you enough stories of things going wrong—whether it's the angler's fault, the fish's fault, or just plain bad luck—to fill three books. It's just part of the game. And just like any other game, the more you play it, the better it seems to get.

As you read through the chapters of this book, you will come upon the word *usually* a great deal. There are no real hard, set rules when it comes to muskies. It comes down to what they *usually* do in a certain situation. They are usually here this time of year, they usually eat when they are that aggressive-looking, they usually like this moon phase. All are perfect examples, but none of them are written in stone. It's muskie fishing and there are no rules, just really good observations and educated guesses. When all the planets align, the muskie plays nice, you strip-strike like your life depends on it, and you win the battle and it is pure magic. You hold the fish for your grip-and-grin, and the grin is the best part of the experience. You probably worked your butt off and experienced a ton of frustration and some failures, but that is all forgotten in the prize at hand. That is why we muskie fish. When you hold a true trophy that not a lot of anglers have experienced while fly fishing, all is forgotten—you are the victor and your hard work and perseverance has paid off in something you will never forget.

The goal of this book is to provide the reader with the basics of the muskie-on-the-fly game. Nothing is more important than time on the water. One can read, study, watch videos, and scan social media, but nothing can prepare you for your first visual muskie eat. As outdoor writer Bill Stokes wrote in his short story "To Shoot a Musky," "I once heard him say that his biggest kick was putting one of those city dudes so close to a charging muskie that the fisherman had to concentrate on his sphincter muscles to avoid acute embarrassment." There's nothing that can prepare you for that first eat. It is experience on the water that truly teaches. Studying is great, but you must spend as much time on the water as you possibly can to really learn. I have hopefully shrunk the basic learning curve for the reader a little. The rest is up to you. Apply a few simple lessons and get on the water and learn. All that any author or guide can do is hopefully point you in the right direction.

This book draws on some of the things I have learned from others and hours of time on the water. If someone says they are a muskie expert, I simple nod my head and move on. No such creature exists. There are plenty of talented anglers and guides that have been chasing muskies a lot longer than I have. I have learned a great deal from a lot of them in the small muskie circle that exists here in the Upper Midwest.

Friend and legend Brad Bohen
AARON OTTO

I don't think that the anglers and guides today show enough respect and gratitude to the men and women that came before them. I'm guilty of that too. In today's world of Instagram and Facebook, with its instant gratification and seeing how many likes or follows we can get, it's nice to look back at the gentle souls and characters that helped pave the way in this crazy world of fly fishing. Seems like more and more folks just want to be the star in their own movie. All I can say is respect the fish and the folks that taught you something about this crazy game. The older I get, the more appreciative I am of all those that helped me along the way and made it possible to make a living guiding and fly fishing. The muskie world wouldn't be the same without colorful characters like Louie Spray, Cal Johnson, Bill Sherer, Brad Bohen, Gil Hamm, and many others. These anglers helped pave the way and provided a rich history for the sport.

The muskie's unpredictability is what makes them special along with the anglers that chase them. You might be able to pattern them at certain times of the year, but no one will ever fully figure them out. If you did, that would take all the fun and intrigue out of it. You will never stop learning or stop being amazed by these fish, and that is what keeps me coming back to them year after year.

CHAPTER TWO

BIOLOGY AND DISTRIBUTION

If you are going to hunt something, it is important to know as much about your prey as possible. Muskie fishing is hunting, especially for the trophy fish. There just aren't many big trophy-class muskies swimming around out there. How do I know that? I know because I have studied their biology. The more you know about a species' biology, the easier it becomes to catch them. Muskies are never easy to catch, but knowing about their biology will take a lot of the guesswork out of it. The main thing that a muskie is concerned with is staying alive and making more muskies. It's really not that hard to understand. Our understanding of these behaviors is where the biology aspect comes into play. There are basically four things that I look for when it comes to behaviors surrounding the muskie's survival: They want to make more muskies, they want to eat, they don't want to work hard, and they want to be comfortable. Knowing how they accomplish all of these things is key to understanding them.

MUSKIE IDENTIFICATION

The muskie is a member of the pike family (Esocidae). They are the top predator in freshwater in the Great Lakes region. They are piscivores, meaning their diet is primarily other fish. Though they look somewhat similar to northern pike and share many similarities, muskies tend to achieve larger sizes than their pike cousins. This simple fact is what draws a lot of anglers to pursue them. Just like the shark fisherman in the ocean, the muskie angler loves to chase the fish that sits on top of the food chain. The other thing that draws anglers is their size. Muskies can reach lengths of over 50 inches and weights above the 50-pound mark. To land a fish that big on a fly rod is not a simple task. If you are muskie fishing, you have to be up to the challenge.

The difference between a northern pike and a muskie is pretty easy to see if you know what to look for. The first thing to look at is the markings on the fish. Muskies have vertical markings versus the horizontal lines of a pike. Muskies can be somewhat difficult to identify by their marking because they have three distinct color phases. They can either be spotted, barred, or clear (silver). Muskies that call the upper Mississippi watershed and the Great Lakes home are generally spotted. The muskies of the inland lakes in the Upper Midwest are generally barred or clear. Markings can sometimes be hard to figure out, but there are two other ways to tell the difference between a pike and muskie. A muskie's tail is deeply forked, making a V shape, while a pike's is more rounded. The most reliable way to tell the difference is by the number of pores that the fish has on the underside of its jaw. A muskie will have six or more, while a northern pike will have five or less.

Some states stock the hybrid known as the tiger muskie, which is a cross between the muskie and the northern pike. They have the rounded tail of the pike, but their barred and spotted markings make them look more like a muskie.

THE SPAWN

The entire muskie fishing year is set up with the spawn. Like most spring-spawning fish, the rest of the year on the water revolves around the spawn. It is the first major event in the muskie's year if we look at it from the fishing calendar. Here in the Upper Midwest, our fishing season starts, for the most part, after the spawn (consult your local fishing regulations for season dates). This is to protect the fish during the spawn and promote a good recruitment of young fry. If you see spawning fish, leave them alone and let them do their thing. If the season is open during the spawn where you are fishing, please practice restraint. The future of the sport relies on fry and small muskies. Let them make more in peace. It's just the right thing to do.

Muskies spawn in the spring in shallow water. They will find a shallow bay or cove that has old weed growth or wood and has warmed up more than the water surrounding this cover. Spawning occurs around 55 degrees Fahrenheit. When the water reaches the high 40s to 50-degree mark, the muskies begin to move into the shallows and stage for the spawn. The females and males pair up and can sometimes be seen swimming in the shallows as if they were glued to each other. The bigger fish in the pair is always the female, and this holds true throughout the years. They do their dance until it is time to spawn. Muskies don't make a bed or nest like that of a bass. The eggs are simply scattered in the shallow water and are usually deposited over submerged, woody debris or other vegetation. If the eggs fall into poor habitat, their survival rate may be low. The eggs need a sufficient amount of dissolved oxygen to survive.

In some waters where pike are also present, they may outcompete muskies due to the fact that they spawn very early. When the muskie fry hatch, the pike fry are already big enough to eat them. Research here in Minnesota revealed an interesting fact regarding this phenomenon. It found that in lakes that held high populations of pike and the pike and muskies shared spawning grounds, the muskies would spawn in slightly deeper water. The presence or absence of pike also seems to affect the ultimate growth rates of muskies. Muskies living in waters that *don't* have a pike population seldom reach lengths of more than 40 inches, but if pike are present in the watershed, muskies can reach lengths surpassing 60 inches. A 40-pound female can produce as many as 200,000 eggs. So, the bigger muskies produce more eggs and help with recruitment of the young. Nature is pretty amazing when you stop and think about it. After the young muskies hatch, they absorb their yolk sac and begin feeding on zooplankton. When they reach a length of around 2 inches, they begin to look for other fish to feed on. They start eating smaller minnows and may even turn to other muskies to keep them sustained.

POST-SPAWN/SUMMER

After the spawn, which can be pretty rough for the females, it takes a bit of time to recuperate from the rigors of the spawn. The fish are often cut up and sometimes even have gouges taken out of them. If you catch a large female during the post-spawn period, it can look as if it just finished an MMA fight. Some fish remain in the shallows for a period of time after the spawn. They will consume almost anything during this time. Post-spawn can be a very productive time of year. In rivers, muskies tend to stay in quieter water so they don't have to work that hard after the rigors of the spawn. They'll eat crayfish, frogs, ducklings, and fish of any species. There is plenty of food in the shallows, and the temperatures are favorable for recuperation and growth. On larger lakes, the bigger fish will often migrate to the main lake basin and follow bait balls around. They gorge themselves on these easy meals to recuperate, and for the fly angler this can be a daunting proposition. They're nomads that follow bait and have no real structure that they relate to. As soon as the shallow water becomes too warm or fishing pressure is heavy, the fish that remained in the shallows after the spawn will slide out of the shallows and start setting up on their summer homes. Deeper weed lines, humps, drop-offs, and rock points can all be spots where the fish will relocate during the warm summer months.

The optimum growth-rate temperature for a muskie is 73 degrees Fahrenheit compared to a northern pike's 66 degrees. They will seek out these optimum temperatures. This is something to keep in mind when fishing in the summer months. In rivers, the fish will follow two things: bait and water temps. During the dog days of summer, muskies will hold in fast water that is well oxygenated and cooler. This type of water holds a lot of bait in the summer too. Redhorse suckers can be found in shallow rocky water, and if that is the case, the muskies will not be far away. If cool riffle water is hard to find in a section of a river, look for springs that will supply both oxygen and cooler water. Muskies will spend most of the summer on these spots and rarely move from them unless something drives them out. Food sources, a bigger fish,

Bob White with a summertime river muskie
MIKE DVORAK

fishing pressure, and water temperatures can all be factors that determine whether a fish stays in its current summer home or seeks a new location. Keep an eye on these situations—they can be helpful when fishing.

Muskies' growth rates fluctuate depending on water temperatures and forage, but they tend to grow rapidly their first few years. The average growth rate is about 6 inches per year until they're 4 years old or so. Once they reach 4 years of age, their growth rates slow substantially, to about 2 inches per year. These growth rates aren't set in stone and can vary depending on food supply and other factors. In a healthy watershed a muskie should reach the 40-inch mark in about twelve years. Once they hit the magic 40-inch mark, their growth rate slows even more, to about 1 inch per year. So, you can see that a 50-inch fish is a special creature. Of course, all growth rates depend on genetics and environmental conditions. Every watershed is different. If you're looking for a true trophy watershed, do your research.

FALL/WINTER

As the summer wears on and the days become shorter, muskies can sense the impending doom of winter. The change in the sun's angle (photoperiodism) and cooler water temperatures tell a muskie that winter is approaching and it needs to strap on the feed bag. They need to feed heavily to nourish the eggs that they will be laying in the spring and to build up reserves for the long winter. This, in many muskie anglers' opinion, is the number one time to chase large females. I tend to agree. I concentrate most of my muskie fishing in the prime fall time period. I start concentrating on them here in the Upper Midwest around the end of September and go until the ice forces me off the water.

Muskies still feed in the winter, but it is nothing like the fall. The dropping water temperatures and shorter days trigger the fish to once again move into shallower water to hunt. They will often also set up on a break line adjacent to their spring spawning areas and will winter there until the spawn urge kicks in during spring. In rivers they will hold in deeper runs, pools, and woody structure where the redhorse or other baitfish winter. They are in safe, deep water with little current and a ton of food nearby—a perfect spot for a big, fat fall muskie. They don't expend too much energy in the cold water in these wintering holes, and with ample food nearby, they don't have to travel far to find their next meal. They will ride these spots out all winter until the cycle starts all over again in the spring.

Knowing this simple biology can help you determine where a muskie is calling home during the different parts of the season. Experience on the body of water that you fish will help you fine-tune these movements from year to year. Just know that every year is different and that nothing is ever written in stone when it comes to muskies.

DISTRIBUTION

Muskies were originally not a very widespread species. With the use of stocking and better management of the species, we have seen more and more states develop fishable populations. As of this writing, thirty-three states have muskies. This number will likely grow as states look to introduce the species into different waters. Anglers have driven a lot of this growth. States that have native species are already seeing the push to introduce muskies to more waters. This can sometimes be a political football, as we have seen in Minnesota over the last few years. Oftentimes, one group of anglers is pitted against another. Here in Minnesota, walleye anglers think that muskies eat all the walleyes, and muskie anglers think walleye anglers control the state. I have even heard trout anglers blaming muskies for the loss of trout populations in a certain river out West. I think everyone just needs to calm down and let the biologists guide those decisions, based on science.

In 2011 a study was done by the Ontario Ministry of Natural Resources and their biologist Steve Kerr, titled "Distribution and Management of Muskellunge in North America." It is a fascinating look into the growth of muskies in North America and their history. Kerr was one of the leading biologists in the field and has since retired. The study gathered responses from over fifty states and provinces in North America concerning muskie management and what these jurisdictions were experiencing in their muskie programs. Besides looking at distribution, the study also looked at regulations, stocking programs, management, and many of the issues that face biologists today. Some interesting things really jumped out in this study. The first thing I noticed was how broad the study was. When over fifty states and provinces take part in a study, you can really get a sense of what each one is doing and how they are looking at their muskie programs. A lot of different views were expressed, and many states and provinces were trying to accomplish different goals. It was interesting to read about these varying aspects of management.

Another observation was that the Upper Midwest and Ontario are still the hot bed for muskie fishing. Distribution of muskies continues to grow, but as of 2011 there were 1,866 muskie waters in North America. The majority of the muskies, 80 percent, are found in just five jurisdictions: Minnesota, Wisconsin, Ontario, Michigan, and West Virginia. With all the talk of stocking and the growth of muskie fishing, that number did surprise me a bit. I know that the Upper Midwest has historically been the muskie capital, but the 80 percent number really did jump out at me. I guess I'm lucky to live where I do.

In the study it also said that 73 percent of North American muskie waters are sustained by natural reproduction. That is also a big number, and it is nice to see that much natural reproduction in our water here in North America. That doesn't mean that muskies don't have issues. The loss of habitat and good spawning areas is a big issue that biologists are facing today. Making sure that we have quality waters in the future for muskies to survive is something we as muskie anglers need to be aware of.

In North America, 46 percent (864) of muskie waters are a result of the introduction of the species into new waters. This is another great number. If you look at the natural reproduction numbers and the introduction numbers, you can clearly see that there is a lot of natural reproduction going on in the waters that muskies were introduced in.

Of the 1,866 current muskie waters, only 493 of them are dependent on stocking to keep a viable population going. The stocking of fish expands muskie fishing opportunities for every angler and has opened the door to a lot of water that normally wouldn't have this great fish. In 2010 almost a million fish were stocked in North America. Stocking is a very expensive proposition. According to the 2010 Wisconsin muskie stocking strategy report, the cost of getting a fish to the age of 18 months varies depending on what size of fish are stocked. The older the stocked fish are, the better the recruitment is to the 18-month mark. As you can see in the chart below, even at $27.42 for one fish to make it to 18 months in the best-case scenario, it is still expensive. Multiply that times 2,000 yearlings, and you're looking at a cost of $54,840. Of those 2,000 fish, four to six will make it to the magic 50-inch mark. Using a best-case scenario, let's say eight make it to 50 inches. That would mean that each one of those fish costs just a bit under $7,000 for a single 50-incher. That's a pretty high sticker price, but for the dedicated muskie angler, it's a price they'd pay every day for a fish that big and special. These numbers will certainly fluctuate due to outside factors, but even if they do, you can see the expense involved in raising one single 50-inch muskie.

Muskie anglers have been more than willing to pitch in and pay for muskie stocking throughout the years. Conservation groups like Muskies Inc. have volunteered their time and funds to help defer the cost of stocking programs. The best thing that has grown over the years from these groups is the strong catch-and-release ethic. Muskie anglers are one of the strongest groups of anglers out there that practice catch-and-release. They are ardent supporters of it. I know for a fact that state record

Wisconsin Muskie Stocking Strategy Numbers for 2010

SIZE OF MUSKIES STOCKED	PRODUCTION COST PER FISH	SURVIVAL RATE AT 18 MONTHS	NUMBER STOCKED/ SURVIVED	COST PER SURVIVOR AT 18 MONTHS
Fry	$1.36/1,000	0.00017%	588,235	$800
Fall fingerlings	$2.83	4%	25	$70.75
Spring yearlings	$5.21	19%	5	$27.42

fish have been caught and released. The thought of killing one of these grand creatures is something that isn't even considered. Records aren't as important as keeping the resource thriving. Seasoned muskie anglers know the cost involved. I think that is one of the reasons for such a strong catch-and-release ethic. They also know how rare a truly giant muskie is. There just aren't a lot of those big muskies swimming around.

Another interesting observation was how the different states and provinces are shaping their management of muskie populations to meet their anglers' expectations. As the growing catch-and-release ethic emerges, anglers are looking for bigger fish. Through the different agencies' input, we have learned that most anglers are looking for a trophy fish experience. Here in Minnesota, the Department of Natural Resources is now managing more for trophy fisheries. They have listened to muskie anglers, and this is the direction that anglers have said they would like to go. In this

Resource managers are the real super heroes of muskie anglers. Their tireless work insures that the resource is protected and thriving.
MINNESOTA DEPARTMENT OF NATURAL RESOURCES, REPRINTED WITH PERMISSION

type of fishery, the goal is to have four to ten fish per acre. One of the more popular muskie lakes here in Minnesota is a little over 110,000 acres. If you do the math, you're looking at a fishery that will hold around 18,000 adult muskies. This is shaping how and where anglers fish. The biology of muskies is being studied by more and more anglers every year. If you want to catch a trophy muskie, you need to know where they live and how they grow. Some watersheds just can't raise big muskies (50-plus inches). If a large muskie is your goal, you need to know where they are growing and how they are being managed. Most big muskies grow in bigger water with a good source of large and fatty bait available. If your goal is to simply catch a muskie on the fly, there are a ton of options for you. Big muskies, as we have said over and over, are very rare. So, figure out your goals. Make a game plan to accomplish your goals by looking at the biological statistics. Then gear up and go for it.

Not everyone is as fascinated by the biology of the muskie as much as I am, and I get that. I will say, however, that it has made me a much better fishing guide and angler. Someone once said to keep your friends close and your enemies closer. After you have chased these creatures a long time, they might turn into an enemy or at least a formidable adversary.

TIPS FOR THE ANGLER FROM A LEADING MUSKIE BIOLOGIST

I spoke with the head of fisheries for northeast Minnesota, Chris Kavanaugh, and asked him what muskie anglers should know from a biologist's point of view. What he said was very interesting:

1. A large muskie is pretty old. Now, it depends on all kinds of factors, but that being said, a 50-inch muskie is pushing 20-plus years old. Getting a true age on a fish is pretty difficult unless you kill it. The jawbone is really the best way to age a fish, and the only way you can get to it is by killing the fish. New stocked fish are now getting sensors imbedded in them that will provide true growth rates and survival data. Technology is going to shed a lot of light on the species for years to come. As I have stated time and again, a large muskie is a special animal.

2. What makes muskies that old is their growth rate. They grow pretty quickly until they reach around the 40-inch mark. Once they reach this mark, their growth rate slows down pretty drastically. There are some lakes that Chris spoke of where growth rates can sometimes only be a centimeter a year, while on other lakes a larger fish can grow from 1 to 2 inches per year.

3. Big muskies don't eat as much as most people think. Chris had a great analogy: Think of a 40-inch muskie as a young, growing, teenaged boy who is playing a lot of sports. That teenaged boy never seems to stop eating. He is growing like a weed, burning a lot of energy in his activities, and needs to keep the furnace

running. A young muskie is the same way. It needs to eat. Now think of an older person. They just don't eat like that. If they do, they need to go take a nap. A large muskie is the same way. It just doesn't need to eat like it once did due to the fact that its growth has drastically slowed down.

4. Many anglers think that muskies will eat a lake out of all the fish. This battle has been going on forever and will probably go on for a lot longer. A lake has only so much carrying capacity. If the muskies really did eat all the walleyes and bass, they would then die themselves. The science just doesn't support this argument. Muskies like soft-fleshed bait. You'll hear stories of anglers having a muskie bite off their walleye or bass as they try to land it. They use this as evidence that muskies eat a lot of other gamefish. I'm not going to say they never do, but they simply aren't a substantial part of their diet. That walleye or bass is just a struggling fish and looks like an easy meal. Think of it as a coyote running to the sound of a wounded rabbit. That's an easy meal, and the coyote is going to come and check it out. A muskie is just doing the same thing. That's what we are trying to imitate with our flies: a wounded baitfish that is an easy meal.

One final word about the people that study these wonderful fish. Natural resource professionals who work tirelessly to ensure that future generations of anglers have a quality experience are true heroes in my mind. Their dedication to all of our resources is a blessing to those who enjoy them. I have talked to many fisheries managers throughout my career, and all of them have been outstanding. If I need a question answered about a body of water, the management of a fish, or future issues, they are always there with an answer and a helpful hand. If you are new to muskie angling, I can't think of a better place to start than talking to a biologist that handles the area you plan to fish. They manage the waters and know more than I'll ever know about the resource and the fish that swim there. It will be time well spent, and they are more than willing to provide you with any help they can. This goes for all species. They are perhaps the best resource an angler has.

Kip Notes

- There aren't a lot of large muskies. You should treat your muskie fishing as if you were big-game hunting. Whitetail archery hunters are notorious for studying their prey. Treat muskies the same way. Learn as much as you can about them and their habits.
- The biology of the muskie teaches us that they are predictable and can be patterned. This is by far the biggest tactic of them all.
- With time on the water these patterns will begin to show themselves. The great thing about them is that they are repeated year after year.
- Remember the four keys: Muskies want to make more muskies, eat, not work too hard, and be comfortable. This is a great place to start figuring out their patterns.
- The key to being a successful muskie angler is finding the fish and feeding them. It is really that simple. No one said it was easy, just simple.

CHAPTER THREE

EQUIPMENT AND RIGGING: FISH IT TILL YOU FIND IT

"Fish it till you find it." What the heck does that mean, you ask? Just what it says. Keep fishing different rods, lines, leaders, and anything else you might use until you find the absolute best setup for you and your budget. No one knows your style better than you. You're the final decision-maker. Don't just settle for something because I, a shop owner, or a friend says that this is what you need. Fish something and then make a wise and informed decision before you plunk down your hard-earned money. So, you are asking how do I do that without breaking the bank? There are several ways. Any good shop owner will let you try something at the shop before you buy. Ask someone that you trust. I loan out a lot of rigs throughout the year. Many clients also try new setups while they're out fishing with me. If there is a will, there is a way. Just don't throw up your hands and not try to figure it out.

Throughout the years, I have probably had more questions on this topic than any other. What's the best rod, what line do you like in this situation, what's your favorite fly, what knot do you find works best, fluorocarbon or wire, snap or direct tie to the fly—all these questions keep popping up and they will continue. I have changed my mind on several topics over the years. People are always looking for the perfect setup and rigging. I don't know if such a thing exists. The technology in the industry is always changing and getting better. The manufacturers in this relatively small niche of a small industry continue to develop new and exciting products that will only help to serve anglers in the future.

I have been fortunate enough to be asked to help develop different equipment over the years. The best part of going through these processes is that these companies

Rigged and ready to go
JON LUKE

are truly listening to the people that use the products every day. Manufacturers in the fly-fishing industry are gear geeks just like most fly anglers. Their passion for the sport and development of new and better products is exciting. So, as you read this chapter, know that things are always changing. What you read today might not be the case a year or two from now. I guess I'm saying, take everything with a tiny grain of salt, because who knows where we'll be five years from now. Look at everything in this chapter like you would if you were buying a new set of tools. The equipment in muskie fly fishing should be considered tools and are made to do the job more efficiently and effectively. Keep searching until you find the tools that fit you best. Remember, you're buying what's best for you, not what someone else thinks you should have. As always, "Fish it till you find it."

FLY RODS

I don't think anything in the fly-fishing world generates more opinions and loyalties than a fly rod. All you have to do is jump on any message board on the internet having to do with fly fishing, and there is always the token question: Which fly rod is best for chasing Tibetan tiger trout? Just watch the opinions and biases fly. Sometimes you'd think they were asking how to achieve world peace. I always get a kick out of these questions. There really isn't a right answer. Remember, opinions are just that, opinions.

Muskie on the fly is a fairly new endeavor in the grand scheme of fly fishing. Most muskie fly rods are just converted saltwater fly rods, though manufacturers are starting to take the muskie angler more seriously as the market continues to grow. They are working with seasoned muskie anglers and getting a better view of what it takes to make a successful fly rod. The best thing that rod designers are doing is actually fishing. They are getting on the water, fishing, asking and seeing what we are doing and how we're fishing. I think that experience goes a long way toward discovering what it really takes to make a quality muskie fly rod.

I have talked and fished with Shawn Combs, Orvis's chief rod designer. We discussed his approach to fly rod design and muskie fly rods in particular. I think it was a great experience for both of us. It was interesting to see both our points of view. For a guide, it was interesting to

Orvis's Pete Kutzer with a quality muskie and the H3 fly rod
GABE SCHUBERT

hear how fly rods are designed and what it takes to go from a concept to a finished product on a fly shop rod rack. It's a much more complicated process than I ever thought it was. I think from a rod designer's point of view, it's beneficial to see how different fly rods work in an actual fishing situation, especially in the muskie realm. Most rod designers, I would bet, have never really done a whole lot of hard-core muskie fishing. Picking up different rods and fishing them in real-life situations is very beneficial for them. Shawn welcomed my input, and I think it really opened his eyes to what was needed when it comes to muskie fly rods. I got a great perspective on just how difficult it might be to find the muskie fly rod Holy Grail.

My first muskie fly rods were just 10- to 12-weight saltwater rods outfitted with a sinking line of some kind. They got the job done, but they had their limitations. A lot of manufacturers tried to launch different kinds of predator rods, but they all had different limitations. Some were short, some had a softer action, some were pool cues with no feel at all, and some casted great but then didn't perform next to the boat on the figure eight. Most rods still do have some type of limitation. The Holy Grail, as I spoke of, just hasn't landed in my hands yet. Now, it might have landed in some angler's hands because we all have our own preferences. What I'm looking for might not be what you are looking for in a muskie rod.

Fly rods are a very personal thing. What might be good for me might not be for you. I might have had a terrible experience with brand X and someone else will think it is the greatest fly rod ever made. I find it humorous that in the fly-fishing world, brand X is the best thing since sliced bread, but as soon as brand Y offers the guide or angler a better deal or it is added to their pro staff, all of a sudden brand Y is the best thing. Just be careful who you are listening to and know that prejudices exist. I have mine too, but I'm also not blind to what is happening in the market-place, nor should you be. Find what works for you and use it without hesitation, and don't pay any mind to someone else's agenda. It comes down to your casting ability and style more than anything. I'm not going to tell you which rod to buy, because I have been proven wrong time and time again. I will help you determine what questions you should ask before you buy a rod. I will stress this over and over again: You can't buy a fly rod without trying it on the water in a fishing situation to really see if it fits you. You can cast a fly rod on the grass or in a gym, but it is never the real deal. Fly rods are made to fish, and unless you fish them, how do you know they will perform for *you*?

What to Look for in a Muskie Fly Rod

1. What Weight Rod?

There are many opinions on this topic. Let me be clear: You can catch a muskie on almost any size fly rod. Muskies aren't prolific fighters. A large, 50-inch muskie will certainly bend your fly rod and can test even the most experienced angler. It's a large fish, and any fish that big will certainly give you a good fight, but it isn't going to be a long, drawn-out affair. The biology of a muskie is much like that of a jaguar. They're built for quick strikes and kills. They're sprinters, not marathon runners.

I look at the selection of a properly sized fly rod as I would a tool. What size hammer do you need to drive that nail into a board? A muskie fly rod is the same thing. Think of a muskie fly as a nail. The bigger the nail, the bigger your hammer needs to be. Here in the Upper Midwest we throw a lot of larger flies—some of them can be up to 20 inches long. A lighter-weight rod isn't going to get the job done over the long haul with the larger flies. Your elbow will end up in pieces. Do you need to throw those large flies? Absolutely not. You need to throw what is best for you. (We'll get into fly selection and size in the following chapter.)

Most muskie anglers choose a 10-weight rod, and you really can't go wrong with that choice. My personal and guide rods are mostly 12-weight rods. I throw some very large flies. I believe in them, and I know they attract larger fish. I know that most people think a 12-weight fly rod is big, heavy, and cumbersome. This takes us back to the technology issue. A high-end 12-weight rod today is lighter and more responsive than they have ever been. I can pick up one of my older 10-weights and it is about the same weight as my newer 12-weights. I can throw pretty much any fly on the 12-weight. It's easier to go up on weight than down. Why struggle casting larger flies if you don't have to? You can throw a wider variety of flies and lines with a larger-weight rod than a lower-sized rod. I like to have as many arrows in my quiver as I can, and a larger fly rod does that. I also feel that a larger fly rod is just more durable than the smaller ones. Muskie fishing is a tough game and can be very hard on your equipment. I think using a larger fly rod is more of a mental thing. I try not to tell my clients the size of the rod so that the misconception of a big, heavy rod doesn't creep into the angler's head.

Now, it still comes down to the angler's comfort zone. Fish what works best for you and the style you like. I just think that you should keep an open mind when looking at different-sized fly rods. Test them, fish them, and remember that there are many ways to fish muskies on the fly. Casting different rods and fishing different setups might open a door to a new way of hunting muskies.

2. Rod Length

I'm not going to say much about rod length. It is more of a personal preference, which is what all rod selection should be about. Here it comes, the *but*. I personally like a longer rod, specifically a standard 9-foot rod with a 4- to 6-inch fighting butt. Why, you ask? Well, there are three main reasons.

First, the longer rods get the fly a little farther away from the angler. I have had the not-so-pleasant experience of watching a 6/0 muskie fly get driven through a client's finger. Let's just say I don't get excited by much, but that one did it. I like to keep those big flies as far away from me and my clients as I can.

The second advantage is that the longer fighting butt can be leveraged against your arm to aid in the cast. It helps reduce fatigue. It is almost an extension of your arm when properly gripped and cast.

The third reason is that I like the longer fighting butt when it comes to figure eights. It gives me a little more control over the process and also helps with fatigue. You put a lot of pressure on your arm and back when you're doing the figure eight after each cast, and any way to reduce that strain is welcome. Now, muskies don't get too spooked by much, but why give them a chance? If I see a muskie following my fly, I like to reach the rod as far out as I can and direct it away from me and the boat. I have seen what I can only describe as direct eye contact with a following muskie. I am watching the fish follow, and as it gets close it can seem as though it is looking away from the fly and directly at you, locking eyes and saying, "Not this time, buddy." It slowly swims away, and you feel utterly defeated. Now, if I can move the fly so that the fish is looking away from the boat and me, I might have at least a better chance of triggering it to eat. Remember, it's the little things that separate the great angler from the good.

**John Gierach putting a
bend in the rod**
MIKE DVORAK

3. Action

There is not a more personal view on fly rod selection than action. Everyone's casting style is different—that is why there are so many different styles of fly rods. I can't tell you which is best for you. You're probably sick of hearing this, but cast different rods to find out. I prefer a faster action for fly manipulation on figure eights, handling heavy sinking lines, and casting in adverse conditions. The action plays into the entire rod. If you like a softer rod, you will most likely be giving something up when it comes to working the figure eight. If you like a super-fast-action rod with a stiff butt section, you will most likely give up some feel and accuracy. This is what Orvis rod designer Shawn Combs and I have talked about as the Holy Grail.

Most of the casting that I do is a slight tap and go. I make a backcast and let the fly briefly touch the water and fire forward. I have found that this is the most effective way to teach new clients muskie casting and also limit the fatigue factor. For this type of casting I need a stiff rod to propel the fly with the high amount of power transfer. Here is the rub: This type of casting isn't the most accurate, and there is not a whole lot of feel to it. The perfect rod, in my opinion, is one that I can tap and go about 85 to 90 percent of the time, but if I needed to make a very accurate cast next to a logjam, I could do that as well. Trying to blend all of that into one rod is a tall order, just ask Shawn Combs. The technology is developing and hopefully in the not-too-distant future we'll all be fishing with the Holy Grail of muskie fly rods.

Here in the Upper Midwest there are plenty of adverse conditions in late fall and early winter. A faster rod just seems to battle these conditions a bit better than a slower one. The extra power they provide seems to drive the fly through the wind and ice better. Now, if you live in an area where weather is not as big a factor as in the Upper Midwest, you might be better off with a softer action. Remember, you are big-game hunting and you want to make sure you have a big enough gun to get the job done.

4. Close Combat

Most muskies are caught close to the boat throughout the year. How a rod performs in close quarters is a very important factor when choosing a fly rod. Is it easy to handle for close combat? What I mean by this is that every muskie cast must be fished all the way to the boat and turned when it gets there, and you need to be able to maneuver the rod to make this happen. How does it work on a figure eight, picking up for the next cast, and handling stripping into the guides of the rod? These are important questions that you need to answer. One thing to keep in the back of your mind is that the fly rod will never be able to set a hook properly. The angler still has to strip-set no matter how close in the fish eats.

What are some of the things to look for? I like a stiffer tip section so it is easier to turn a fly under the water. There is less give on the tip section, making it easier to manipulate the fly underwater. I want to be able to move it any way I want when I'm trying to trigger an eat from a muskie following my fly.

I like a bigger fighting butt to help me spin a fly on a figure eight. That little bit of extra control can help turn the fly and also saves your arm and elbow some wear and tear. The larger fighting butt can also help in casting larger flies.

Another thing to look at is the size of the first three guides on the rod tip. On many casts and retrieves, the leader ends up into the first few guides of the rod. I like to have oversize guides on the rod just to make it a little easier to strip the leader into the guides if I need to. They also help get the cast started when the leader is into the guides. I have at times taken my rods to my local fly shop to have larger tips put on them to eliminate this problem. It makes a day of muskie fishing just a little bit easier and gives me one less thing to worry about.

5. Rod Configuration

The world of fly rods is in a constant state of flux. What is hot this year might not even be in production next year. Muskie fly fishing in the grand scheme of things is still a very young proposition. It has only been in the last twenty years or so that it has really become somewhat mainstream. There are basically three rod configurations that I'll talk about.

First is your basic fly rod, usually a 9-foot rod with a standard smaller fighting butt. This is the same fly rod type that you would use in most saltwater applications. There are probably more options in this category than any other. You can get them in any number of actions, weights, and lengths. They are workhorses and are just fine for today's muskie fishing. I still have many of them in my quiver and they are great tools.

Standard Orvis H3 12-weight
THE ORVIS COMPANY

Next are the Spey-type rods—or, as some folks call them, two-handed rods. Spey casting has been around since the mid-1800s, and it was only a matter of time before anglers incorporated Spey-type methods into muskie fly fishing. Spey-type rods have become a very effective tool for muskie fly fishing. They probably have been used longer than most people think. I had a client a dozen years ago ask me about using them. He was very much into Spey casting and was wondering if I thought it would work on muskie flies. I told him I didn't see why not. That winter he contacted one of the better Spey rod builders out West and told the builder what he was looking for. The angler and builder put their heads together and came up with a very nice rod. It might have been one of the first true Spey-type rods ever solely built for casting muskie flies. He brought it out the next year, and I have to say I was impressed. With very little effort at all, he was able to cast a large muskie fly easily 60 feet. It had a bigger fighting butt than your standard fly rod, which made figure eights easier, and it was fairly fast and longer than your standard fly rod, which made manipulating the fly very easy. The best part of it was the fact that he could cast large muskie flies all day with a lot less effort than it takes with the standard rig. By using two hands you take out some of the wear and tear on your casting arm. Fatigue is definitely less of a factor with this type of rod setup. It was one of those "aha" moments for me. I have seen more and more anglers cast Spey-type rods. It's a great tool, but it does take a bit of practice to really get the casting down. My client's rod wasn't a true Spey rod in the way a rod used for steelhead fishing is. It was built to handle the larger flies and shoot a bigger weight without

Spey-type fly rods can be a very effective tool.
THE ORVIS COMPANY

Orvis Clearwater muskie hybrid rod
THE ORVIS COMPANY

collapsing in the butt section of the rod. Traditional Spey rods tend to have a bit of a softer butt section to deliver line as far as possible, but this would be detrimental in a muskie fly rod. That stiffer butt section is essential for delivering the larger payload that muskie fishing demands.

Finally, as stated earlier, the game is always changing, and now we are getting hybrids that combine the best of both the standard fly rod and the Spey rod. These are what I see as the muskie fly rod of the future. You have the lightness of the new modern fly rods and the effective casting of Spey rods. With the hybrid rods, you get a responsive high-tech rod that is easier to cast and fish. As I said earlier, we are still in the early stages of muskie fishing on the fly. As the sport continues to grow and evolve, manufacturers are going to continue to tweak their offerings for the fly angler. It will be very interesting and exciting to see how things progress in the future.

You can see that there are a lot of things to consider when you're thinking about getting a new muskie fly rod. I'll say it again: You have to fish them to see what feels and works the best for you. Every year it seems that I do at least one show-me float. I will rig up four or five fly rod combinations for each client to try throughout the day. I try to find out as much as I can before selecting the outfits for my clients for the day. Are they experienced fly anglers? What about bigger flies? Experience with sinking lines? Are they going to mainly fish rivers or lakes? What price point are they comfortable with? Hopefully this points me in the right direction so I can let them see what is available. They'll cast the different rods throughout the day to see what works best for them. It is interesting to watch them react to the different setups. More often than not the setup I thought they would gravitate toward is not the one they like the best. It's just more proof of what I have been trying to preach. I can recommend something that I think will work for you, but until you fish it, you'll never know for sure.

Fly line basics: diagram of the parts of a fly line
SCIENTIFIC ANGLERS

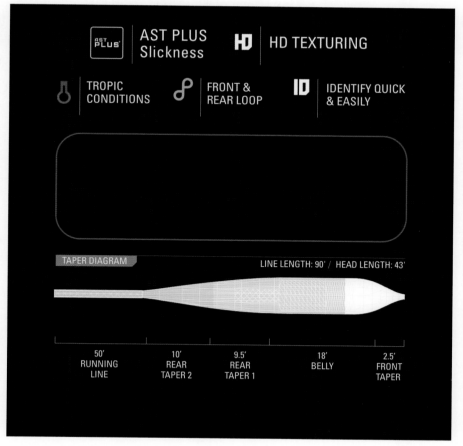

Loading it up
JON LUKE

LINES

If you thought picking a fly rod was complicated, you haven't seen anything yet. Fly lines might be my weak spot when it comes to fly fishing. I believe that the fly line is the most important part of a good fly-fishing outfit. Let me repeat that: The fly line you choose to use is the most important part of a fly-fishing outfit.

I'm always looking for that perfect line to make my fly rods perform at their peak efficiency. Here is a case in point. I was given a new Orvis rod to put through the paces a few years back. I put the line on it that I thought would really make it sing. It did. It was one of the most accurate and easiest casting rods I had ever experienced. The more I fished the fly rod, the more familiar I got with it. I thought that it might be missing a little something—I just felt that I wasn't getting all I could out of it. I called Pete Kutzer at Orvis for a little advice, and he pointed me in a different general direction that I wasn't accustomed to. So, I started messing around with different fly lines on the rod. I probably tried three different lines on it till I found the one that really made that rod sing. It was a great rod before, but I moved it to the next level with just a little adjustment with the fly line. It wasn't much of an adjustment—I just went with the same general line I had on it to begin with. The difference was that the new line had just a little longer belly on it. It made all the difference in the world. That fly rod is now by far one of the best fly rod setups I have ever cast. A good fly line will make a bad fly rod good, and a bad fly line will make a very good fly rod just average.

Casting muskie flies isn't really casting as much as it is chucking flies, especially large flies. The fly line is the main delivery system we rely on to cast these large flies. Muskie flies are super heavy when they get wet. I can cast a large fly with my bait-casting rig at least 40 feet. So, you can see that the weight of the fly itself is enough to make the cast happen. Fly line certainly helps with a cast, but I look more at the overall performance of a line than just its ease in making a cast. If I'm smallmouth bass or trout fishing, I need the weight of the line to deliver an accurate and long cast. That is the number one goal of a fly line in those applications. In muskie fly fishing the picture is a whole lot larger. Let's face it, though—presentation is not something a muskie angler has to be worried about. We just want the fly delivered where we want it at the depth we want it.

I'm most concerned about three things when choosing my fly lines for muskie fishing. The first is whether it will turn over the size of fly I want it to. The second is what depth the line is putting my fly in. The third and probably the one that is most concerning to me is durability. When you are spending that kind of money on fly lines, you want something that is going to last more than just a day or two. Trust me, I have seen lines blow up after just two or three casts. In all fairness, the muskie game is fairly new and perhaps one of the hardest types of fishing on fly lines. The stress that a muskie fly puts on a line is probably a worst-case scenario for any line manufacturer. The line makers are trying to get a better understanding of all the factors that go into casting flies that big. I have worked with some of these R&D teams to try to educate them on what and how we do it. A great deal of progress has been made, and just like fly rods, fly lines will only get better as technologies continue to improve.

Tapers

The advent of heavy weight-forward fly line tapers has probably done more to open up greater opportunities for fly anglers than any other technological advance in the industry. The ability to cast heavy flies longer distances has made fly fishing easier for everyone and has blown the door wide open to the possibilities for all fly anglers. I have seen this take place in all the species that I guide for. My warmwater guiding has changed more due to these taper advances than anything else. We used to have to overline our rods, use saltwater lines, and change line depending on the temperature. It was a real struggle for us in the early days. It seemed like we were always chasing the line. Now I can put a line on at the beginning of the season and pretty much use it for the entire season. I don't have to worry. I just put the line on and fish.

Choosing the right taper is not as hard as it once was. In the muskie game you only really have to worry about one type of taper: It has to be a very aggressive

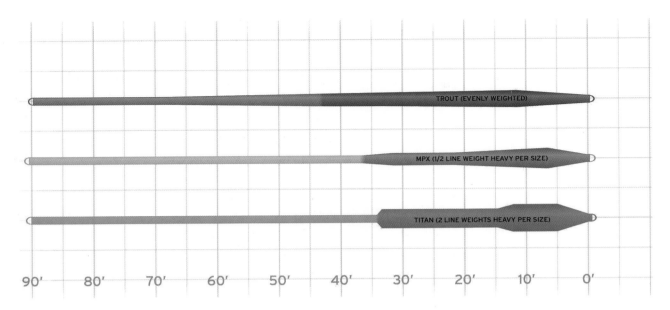

90' 80' 70' 60' 50' 40' 30' 20' 10' 0'

TROUT (EVENLY WEIGHTED)

MPX (1/2 LINE WEIGHT HEAVY PER SIZE)

TITAN (2 LINE WEIGHTS HEAVY PER SIZE)

**Basic fly line
taper designs**
SCIENTIFIC ANGLERS

weight-forward-type line. It comes down to your casting style. Are you a classic caster in the sense of false casting in the air? Do you have a hybrid rod and use the water to help load the rod? Are you using a Spey-type rod and need to have a specific Spey line? These are all factors that will play into a taper. Then comes the size of fly that you will be using. The bigger your flies, the more grains you'll need on the head of your fly line.

Remember what I said about rod size: It's easier to have a bigger stick than a smaller one. The same is true for fly lines. If you don't have enough grains in the head of the fly line, it is very hard to turn over your fly. It's easier to have a heavier line than a lighter one. I use this example a lot in my teaching: I can cast a size 14 Adams on a 10-weight rod if I have to. But I can't throw a 15-inch muskie fly on a 3-weight. It's just not going to happen. You'll most likely break the rod trying to attempt it.

I try to match the line to the rod weight that I am going to use and am comfortable with. This is where line choice begins. Let's use a 10-weight as an example since it is the most common muskie rod size. I begin by looking at lines that match the rod size. Keep in mind that every manufacturer seems to look at all of this a little different than the others. We'll use floating line specifications for the purpose of this example. According to the American Fishing Tackle Manufacturers Association (AFTMA), the proper grain size for a 10-weight line is 280 grains. (Grains are measured in the first 30 feet of a fly line.) If you go and look at heavy weight-forward lines, the grains are very different. For example, a 10-weight Scientific Anglers Mastery Titan line is rated at 380 grains. This line has a very aggressive taper and is what I like when casting larger flies. Keep in mind that even most trout lines are overweighted these days.

Next is the hard part: finding the sweet spot. It depends a lot on your casting style. Everyone has their own style and matches the rod and line to that style. The sweet

Line Weight	Low Weight in Grains	Target Weight in Grains	High Weight in Grains
1	54	60	66
2	74	80	86
3	94	100	106
4	114	120	126
5	134	140	146
6	152	160	168
7	177	185	193
8	202	210	218
9	230	240	250
10	270	280	290
11	318	330	342
12	368	380	392
13	435	450	465
14	485	500	515
15	535	550	585
80			

AFFTA Approved Fly Line Weight Specifications

KIP VIETH

spot is where the rod loads with as little effort as possible and shoots the line with ease. Now, remember it's muskie fishing and that can be a tall order. Casting muskie flies always takes some effort. Making it as easy as possible is our goal. Cast lines in a real fishing situation and find the one that fits your style and rod the best.

If you're new to something, ask someone that you trust and knows what you're after. Don't go on the internet and ask what line will work for a certain rod. You'll get a bunch of answers and will probably end up where you started. You want someone that will give you honest feedback and is not trying to sell you something. Remember what I said about rods, and the same is true about lines: We all have our opinions and prejudices. Find a guide or shop owner that you trust and has experience fly fishing for muskies. Unless you have fished for muskies, it's hard to understand what it takes.

Before I went redfishing for the very first time, I called my guide and asked him what I needed to get the job done. He wasn't trying to sell me anything and just wanted me to be successful. He's been doing it a long time and knows what works for his type of fishing. I followed his advice, and everything worked out splendidly.

Another great resource is the manufacturers. If you have questions about a line that you are interested in, pick up the phone and give them a call. They have people that know their products better than anyone and are more than happy to help you with your questions.

Depth

Another important factor when choosing a line is where in the water column you are going to be fishing. Are you throwing large topwater flies on weed lines during the summer months? Working wood piles and sweepers on rivers? Running deep wintering holes or rock bars? Line selection is key to presenting the fly to a hunting muskie. For the most part, muskie anglers are running a sinking line setup. The larger flies can be very buoyant with the amount of deer hair they have on them, and muskies for a good portion of the season hold in deeper water in both lakes and rivers. Getting the fly into a muskie's neighborhood so that it can eat it is paramount. The only way for the angler to really control this is by fly line choice.

Like the grain weight rating on floating fly lines, sinking fly lines are rated by their sink rates. This helps the angler figure out how deep the line will get their fly. It can be confusing, but I think it is a little easier to understand than the whole grain weight thing. All you really need to know is where in the water column you need to be and try to match the sink rate to that depth.

Muskies usually hunt by looking up. If they see something that interests them, they will swim up and check it out. You don't have to be dragging the bottom when hunting muskies. You just need to get the fly deep enough so they can see it. In the summer, on a lake, the muskies can be in deep weed lines or rock bars 20 or more feet down. You'll need a pretty aggressive sinking line to get your fly into their neighborhood. On the rivers that I fish, there are seldom holes that are more than 10 feet deep. You wouldn't need as aggressive a sink rate as in the lake situation.

Know what kind of situation you'll be fishing in and what type of sinking line you might need. You might not even need a sinking line if you are going to throw a topwater fly. This knowledge will come with time on the water and learning your fishing style. The sink rate chart is a great place to begin to determine how fast a certain line will sink. It's just a reference. There are other factors that you might have to consider when looking at sinking lines, like how just because a line has a sink rate of 5 inches a second doesn't mean that rate is written in stone. A lot of other factors go into how far a fly sinks in any given situation, such as the fly type, currents, and how the angler is moving the fly.

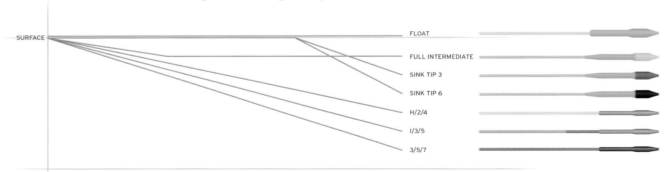

The different sink rates of fly lines
SCIENTIFIC ANGLERS

As mentioned earlier, line manufacturers have started to give the muskie angler a lot of quality choices. They have begun offering multiple-density lines, with different sections that sink at different rates. This helps get rid of a lot of the line sag so that you have more of a direct connection to the fly and the fish when they eat. It has been one of the big steps in line design in the last few years and is a game changer. I typically get a couple of lines a year from the manufacturers to put through the paces to see where more and better improvements can be made to muskie lines in the future.

I have many types of sinking lines for most of the situations that I may encounter during the day. I will often have four rods rigged up with four different types of sinking lines on them. If you fish the same piece of water most of the time, you can probably get away with having just a few. It really comes down to fishing different fly lines to see which one works best for the situation you are in. Just like fly rods, lines are ever-changing, and what will be available in a couple years from now will most likely be vastly better and more effective.

REELS

If you want to save some money on your setup, this is the place to do so. I can probably count on both hands the times that I have had a muskie on the reel. I have a saying: "If the fish wants to get on the reel, he will." Let the fish make the decision for you. It's really that simple.

In all my years of guiding, I have seen more fish lost because the angler was trying to get it on the reel. I've seen it time and again. The angler thinks they need to get the fish on the reel, so they immediately begin reeling like a madman, trying to pick up slack to get tight on the fish. The minute this happens, nine out of ten times the rod tip comes down, slack is put in the line, and the fish says good-bye. Muskie fishing is for the most part close-quarters hand-to-hand combat. They aren't big runners—it's fighting a bulldog next to the boat. The need for a freight-train-stopping drag is just not there. If you're going to use this reel for saltwater or other large running fish, however, get the best drag you can afford.

There are plenty of great reels out there. Once again, the technology keeps getting better and better. Reels just keep getting lighter and stronger. The drag systems that reels have today are simply amazing, as are their finishes, spool configurations, and any number of other options they have. I will say this: I like to have as light of a reel as I can. It just helps with fatigue, and with muskie rigs you don't have to worry much about reel balance. Find what works best for you and run with it. As my grandfather used to say, "They're all good, some's just better than others."

It's hard to write about equipment because everything is changing so fast. As I sit here today and write this, it is simply amazing to think about what will be coming down the line in the future. I can sit here and rattle off all kinds of equipment recommendations for you, but advances will continue to come. Technology is a blessing and a curse. As soon as you think you have it dialed in, something new comes along. Just keep fishing and trying new things. New equipment will keep coming as long as the earth spins around the sun. Keep experimenting, and if you find something that works, fish it; if not, look to a trusted source for guidance. You'll never stay ahead of the equipment curve. It's an endless game that no one ever truly wins. Just remember to fish it till you find it!

Kip Notes

- As I've said, fish it till you find it.
- Everyone has a different casting style. No two anglers' styles are the same. Find yours. What works for me might not work for you. Experiment.
- Keep up with changing technologies as best you can. It can seem like a daunting task. Changes are coming faster and faster. Talk to other anglers and industry people so you can keep a pulse on the changes.
- When setting up a muskie outfit, spend your money in this order: fly line first, rod second, and then the reel.

CHAPTER FOUR

THE BUSINESS END: RIGGING AND TOOLS

Let's get one thing clear: Most fish that aren't landed are due to angler error. The biggest limiting factor to angler success lies between the angler's ears. That will probably never change. It could be a bad hook-set, not performing a proper figure eight, or the lack of concentration. These are some of the bigger factors. The second area where things most commonly come unglued is what I call "the business end." The business end begins at the loop on the end of your fly line and stops at the hook point of the fly. It is basically your leader setup and fly. This is the weakest link in the chain besides the angler, and the angler is by far the weakest link.

A lot more things can go wrong on the business end than anywhere else in the system. Knots can fail, leaders can break, and all kinds of other weird stuff can seem to happen in the business end. When you look at it closer, however, it probably still comes down to human error. Someone didn't tie a good knot, didn't check the leader, didn't secure the snap, or forgot to sharpen the hook. These are huge factors on the business end. Keeping everything running at peak performance will do more for your success than any other thing I can think of. Like I said before, the biggest factor is what is between your ears. If you can keep the business end of the equation strong, the rest will seem to go a little easier. It's just one less thing to worry about.

LEADERS

When it comes to leaders, there are a ton of opinions. There is no right or wrong. Everyone's water is a little bit different, and what works on the Upper Mississippi River might not be what works on the James River in Virginia. I have found this holds true more often than not on most waters all over a good portion of North America.

Remember, you're not fishing spring creek brown trout. I recommend a very short leader for most situations. Muskies aren't leader shy. You'll hear this over and over again in this book: If a muskie wants to eat your fly, he is going to. I like to use a shorter leader to give me more control over what's going on in the business end of my setup. The main reason for this is the figure eight. This is the close combat that we discussed earlier. You need to be able to manipulate your fly as quickly and as effectively as you can in a short period of time. If you're using a 9-foot leader, there is no way that you will be able to turn a proper figure eight. There is just too much leader, and you will be unable to keep the fly moving properly. If the fly stalls, this can often send a muskie heading in the wrong direction. I often use the example of the lion and impala. When a lion chases an impala, the impala doesn't stop running until it is safe or gets eaten. Think of the muskie as the lion and your fly as the impala. If that fly stops because you can't keep it moving due to a long leader, it just doesn't look natural. You need to keep the fly moving and work that fish. The short leader enables you to control your fly and make it do what you want, when you want. You want a direct connect to the rod, and the short leader makes that possible. When the fish does eat, there will be less slack and a better connection to the fish with the shorter leader. A shorter leader, in my opinion, is a better tool for the job.

Bite guards are another topic that a lot of people have opinions about. It is my belief that an angler works too hard to have a fish burn through their bite guard. I'm a firm believer in wire. I have used fluorocarbon in the past and have lost some truly large fish with bite-offs. It isn't a matter of *if* you're going to have one burn through a fluorocarbon leader, it's a matter of *when*. I can honestly say that I have never had a fish break a wire leader. I know a bunch of fluorocarbon users that have switched back to wire due to lost fish. There isn't a worse feeling than losing a fish you have been chasing all season to a bite-off, and the worst part of it is that it was something that you could have controlled. You chose the leader and it is on you. Many things in muskie fishing are out of the angler's control—leader setup isn't one of them. Some muskie anglers will argue that the fish can see the leader and that it will cost you a few fish. It might, but I'd rather lose a few opportunities than an actual fish that has decided to eat my fly. Once again, if a muskie wants to eat your fly, it will. The longer I have done this, the more I've come to realize that. You could have a blaze-orange bite guard and if that muskie's switch is flipped, it is going to eat. There are many wire products on the market, from standard stainless to titanium to hybrids, and they're all good. Find one that you like and are comfortable working with. Use wire and avoid the heartbreak of losing a fish of a lifetime.

Now that I've sung the praises of using a wire bite guard, there is one drawback. Tying a fly to a wire bite guard can be a real pain at times. I'll admit, sometimes wire is not very easy to work with. I try to take some of the pain out of it by using a stay-lok snap on the end of my leader. The reason is that I then usually only have to tie one knot a day. Oh, I might lose a fly to the river or have a bad kink in the wire and then have to tie another snap on, but most days it's one knot and done. I just have to make sure that one knot is secure. I test it several times before I give it my blessing. The fewer knots I tie, the better. It takes some of the human element out of your leader. The snap also allows me to switch out flies faster, especially when working an active fish. If I have an active fish and it has followed but not committed, I can quickly switch flies and present the new fly to it while it is still active. Sometimes giving an active fish something different to look at can trigger an eat. Remember, it's the little things. Another advantage of the snap is that when the temps are in the 30s or colder, I really don't want to be tying knots that much. My hands don't seem to work very well when there are icicles hanging from them. Cold hands don't tie quality knots. The snap goes a long way in this situation.

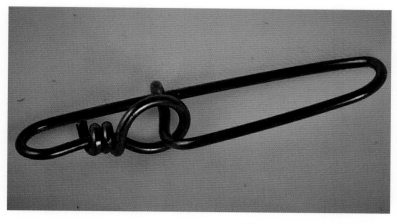

The stay-lok snap is the only snap to use. It prevents the snap from coming apart in the heat of the battle.
KIP VIETH

I will say this: There is only one type of snap to use, and that is the stay-lok type (pictured here). Even if it comes unsnapped for some reason, it has a backup ring that will keep it from coming apart. It is by far the best type of snap out there.

Leader Formula

It's a pretty basic leader that I tie. You can certainly experiment with different lengths, etc., for your own fishing conditions.

I start out with a 60-pound fluorocarbon section of about 30 inches or so. I then cut an 18-inch section of bite guard. I use 45-pound coated stainless steel 1x7 wire. To join the fluoro and the wire, I tie an Albright knot, cinch it down good, and apply a little superglue just to make sure. I then go up to the end of the fluorocarbon and tie a perfection loop to attach to the fly line. I will put a drop of glue on this too. I like the gel-type superglues—they are easier to work with and don't make as much of a mess. Next is the snap. I just tie it on with a three-turn clinch knot. I pull it tight and make sure that nothing is going to slip. After I have tied it all up, I test it over and over. I take my BogaGrip and put the snap on it, and then pull on it to 35 pounds to make sure that nothing is going to give. I do this a couple of times. If it looks like something isn't right, I just tie another one.

If you want to, you can put some shrink tubing over the clinch knot and snap for a little more security. I put a piece of shrink tubing over the area and heat it with a lighter just to add a bit of protection to that important knot. You can also crimp a sleeve on the tag end of the leader for extra security if you wish.

Losing a fish of a lifetime over something you control is inexcusable. Trust me, it has happened to me; just ask my son. I didn't change a leader one morning while I was fishing with him, and it cost him his first big muskie. To top it off, he lost one of Gabe's (Muskie Jesus) prized flies. He was more upset about losing the fly than the fish. He knows how special Gabe's flies are. It also taught me a valuable lesson: It is the little things that will put a muskie in the net. I would just tell you that when it comes to leaders, the devil is in the details. If you have any doubt in your leader, just

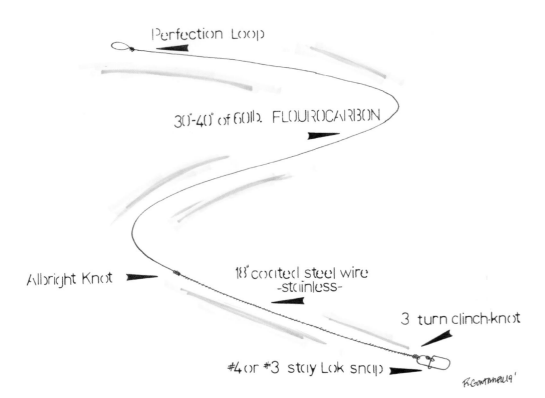

Perfection Loop

30'-40' of 60lb. FLOUROCARBON

The basic leader setup for
most muskie situations
RUSS GRONTAREK

Albright Knot

18' coated steel wire
-stainless-

3 turn clinch-knot

#4 or #3 stay Lok snap

R.GONTAREL19'

change or fix it. Don't get lazy like I did. If there is a weak spot in it, a muskie has a way of showing you the hard way. Take your time, do it right, and triple-check it, and you won't find yourself weeping in the bottom of the boat over a lost 50-inch muskie due to leader failure.

KNOTS FOR MUSKIE FISHING

Knots, love 'em or hate 'em, they're all part of fishing. In muskie fishing, there are just a few that you really have to know. Below is a list of what I consider the essentials. If you know these knots, you have everything you'll need. Everybody has their favorite. I say if you're comfortable with a knot, use it. If I have confidence in a knot, I find I use it more than any other. I know that it works, and I usually tie it better. Chances are that you tie your favorite knot more, and we all know that practice makes perfect.

If you struggle with knots, there are a ton of videos and tutorials out there. One of the best is in the Orvis Fly Fishing Learning Center. I go to this often if I need a refresher on a knot that I'm not as comfortable with as others. The Learning Center is a resource for all kinds of fly-fishing questions you might have. Here is the link to the knot section: https://howtoflyfish.orvis.com/fly-fishing-knots.

- **Perfection Loop:** This is a knot that you have to know. If you use a loop-to-loop system, this knot is a must. It can take a little practice, but once you get it down, it is very easy.

- **Albright Knot:** This is the knot that I use most when tying my wire bite guard to my mono. It is very reliable and not as bulky as some. Not having a bulky knot helps in the event you have to strip the leader into the guides.
- **Basic Clinch Knot:** Probably the most popular knot in all of fishing. It has stood the test of time and is tough to beat. I only twist it three times when tying wire on to a snap.
- **Double Uni Knot:** A great knot when tying two lines together. Just think blood knot, only stronger and easier to tie. It is a little bulkier than some.
- **Nail Knot:** Another oldie but goodie. I use this when tying mono to the fly line if I need to replace the loop on the line.
- **Non-Slip Mono Loop Knot:** I use this knot probably more than any other throughout my entire guiding season. It's a great knot to use when tying on bigger flies to the leader. I use it on all my poppers and streamers if I'm not using some kind of snap system.
- **Arbor Knot:** The go-to knot when tying your backing to the reel.
- **Slim Beauty Hybrid:** Another line-to-line knot that is very strong and fairly easy to tie.

TOOLS FOR THE HUNT

My boat bag has a reputation of being pretty heavy. I've been known to jam everything I can into it depending on the time of year. Leaders, tippets, extra reels, a Jetboil, snaps, my camera, a fly line or two, and a lot of tools—my bag has a ton of stuff and probably more than I need. That being said, there are a few things that you should have at your disposal for muskie fishing.

Hook Sharpener

This might be one of the most important tools that a muskie angler can have. Putting a hook into the hard jaw of a muskie is difficult at best. Having the sharpest hook possible is an absolute must. I try to check my hooks several times a day just to make sure that the hook point hasn't been rounded in the least. Another thing to keep in mind is hook selection for your flies. Some hooks are easier to keep sharp than others. There are several brands of hooks that are very sharp out of the box, but when they do get dull it is almost impossible to put a sharp point back on them. Check the hook on your fly before it even gets wet to make sure it is sharp and ready to go.

Sunglasses

There is a reason I have put sunglasses second in this section—they are that important. This might be the most overlooked tool in all of fly fishing. Yes,

Sharp hooks are a must. Keep them sharp and you will be glad you did.
KIP VIETH

Sunglasses are an often-overlooked but important tool.

KIP VIETH

sunglasses are a tool. Webster defines tool as *something (as an instrument or apparatus) used in performing an operation or necessary in the practice of a vocation or profession.* Now, some would argue that sunglasses just really aren't that important. They are a tool by definition because they are necessary in the practice of a vocation. If you are not fishing with a quality—and yes, I said quality—pair of polarized glasses, you are fishing blind.

Take, for example, the following story. It was the first day of the very first Orvis Muskie School. We had just finished up the classroom portion and were starting the casting part of the school. We gathered on the dock of the resort, and Pete Kutzer started teaching the basics of casting large muskie flies. We had gotten most of the students slinging them pretty good when I took over to show them how to work the flies, figure eights, and strip-setting. It was a cloudy and rainy day, and I was wearing my brown polarized guiding glasses—the ones that I guide in 95 percent of the time. The glare on the water was especially bad that late afternoon. I was having a very hard time seeing into the clear water even with my quality polarized glasses. I was complaining to Pete about them, and he offered me his pair. They had yellow lenses in them and were supposed to cut the glare and make everything a bit brighter on cloudy days. I slipped them on, and it was as if someone had flipped a switch. The entire lake was illuminated. I could see everything and was blown away by the glasses' performance. Needless to say, when I got home, I ordered a pair of low-light sunglasses as quickly as I could. It just cemented my opinion on having a good pair of quality polarized sunglasses. It also taught me a very valuable lesson: An angler should have more than just one pair of sunglasses. Light conditions change often, and having a couple of options can be a game changer.

When muskie fishing is the best, it is often the worst of conditions. Clouds, rain, or snow that puts an unforgiving light on the water can be rough. Having a tool that cuts that glare and lets you see into the water is invaluable. The sooner you can see a muskie following your fly, the sooner you can start working the fish. You can manipulate the fly away from the boat, start your turn sooner, and control the situation just that much better. Muskie fishing is all about taking advantage of all the opportunities that are presented to you. Seeing that fish as soon as possible is one of those opportunities.

I tell my clients to yell "Fish!" as soon as they see one. I am often sitting in the rower's seat and don't have the advantage of seeing as much as they do. If the client can't see the fish and doesn't let me know what's going on, it can often end poorly. I have hit a fish with the oars because neither the client nor I saw it. Now, it's muskie fishing and stupid things seem to happen. The client did, however, show up with a good pair of glasses on the next trip.

The other factor is safety. If you are doing any kind of fly fishing, just wear glasses. A hook in an eye usually doesn't end well. Be safe, wear the glasses. It's a no-brainer when you really stop and think about it. By the way, wear a hat with a bill on it too. It cuts the glare and offers another layer of protection.

Big-Enough Fly Box

Nothing makes me as mad as a fly that I spent three hours tying getting smashed and deformed in a cramped fly box. When I first started chasing muskies, I would just store them in a Tupperware container. After fishing, I would have to pull them out of the container and hang them so they dried the right way. If I forgot about them, the hooks would rust, deer hair would get smashed, and flash and feathers would get twisted. Well, manufacturers finally realized that there was a need for large fly boxes for predators.

One of the best muskie fly boxes available

JON LUKE/JUSTEN CASE

A while back, I was at my local fly show and noticed that Matt Cassel, owner of Cliff Fly Boxes, had a large box sort of hid in the back of the booth. I asked him if he was into bird dogs too. He looked at me kind of strangely and I said, "Why do you have a bird dog collar box in your booth?" He grabbed it and showed me the new prototype box he was working on. I said, "Wow, I've been looking for a box like that forever." It was big enough to hold my muskie and smallmouth flies. It was the answer. At the end of the show, as we were breaking down our booths, Matt came over and handed me the box. I still have it, the original Beast Box by Cliff. They are still great boxes and hold flies very nicely. I still use them.

Just like everything in muskie fly fishing, things have evolved and just gotten better. As flies have gotten bigger and bigger, the need for a better fly box has grown. The Just Encase company here in Minnesota makes a fantastic product. Each fly is hung individually and can dry and stay in perfect form in this box. They don't give them away, but they are bombproof and hold large muskie flies better than anything I have seen. They also come in a lot of different configurations. I'm sure that more and better boxes will come down the pipe. It's also a personal preference, but a good box will pay for itself in keeping your flies dry and in good working order.

Needle-Nose Pliers

A good, long needle-nose is essential. It is key to getting the hook out of a muskie quickly. My goal is to get the fish back in the water as soon as possible. There are a ton of different fishing pliers out there for the fly angler. In my opinion, a pair of old-fashioned long needle-nose pliers from your local hardware store is the best way to go. I like the longer pliers for working hooks out of a muskie's mouth. Keep in mind that muskie flies are large and hairy, making removal difficult at times. There is just a lot going on in a muskie's mouth with a 15-inch deer hair fly and razor teeth waiting to wreak havoc. I like the longer and thinner pliers to get in there and free the fly, and the cutter in the pliers is great for cutting wire and heavy mono for leader building. Another advantage to an Ace Hardware special is that if it gets caught in the net and flips into the water, you're not out $200. Trust me, it has happened to me a couple of times and it's a tough lesson to learn. I never said I was a brain surgeon.

Every tackle bag should have one.
KIP VIETH

Side-Cutter Pliers

Why would I need side-cutter pliers if I already have needle-nose pliers? I have them for cutting hooks and wire. It just makes cutting the bigger stuff a little easier and more efficient. I haven't had to do it often, but cutting a big muskie hook is a possibility. I even had to take a hook out of a client once. Hopefully that will be the last time. When a client is looking at his hand with a 15-inch fly and 6/0 hook hanging from it, you'll be glad you have the bigger side cutters. I have also on several occasions had to cut the hook when a muskie was hooked in a very difficult position. It's often easier to just cut the hook than sacrifice a muskie for your fly. Cut the hook and let the muskie live.

Superglue

Superglue has saved my bacon more than a few times over the years. The situation I use it most for is to secure my knots when I'm making my leaders. I'm just a little more confidant in my leaders if I throw a drop or two on my knots. It gives me a bit more security.

I've used superglue for all kinds of other things too. I have often used it to make quick repairs on flies after a fish tore them up a bit. It can be used to make a quick repair on a fly line or sink tip if need be. I have made emergency rod repairs with it. I've even used it for some first-aid issues that have arisen in the boat. It's just a great thing to carry in your boat bag for a day of fishing.

BogaGrip

BogaGrips have taken a lot of grief on social media over the last few years. If used properly, they are a great tool. Please don't use them to lift a fish. You can break a large muskie's back or break their jaw. Lots of people want to weigh their fish. Just don't do it. You really risk hurting or killing them by lifting them with a BogaGrip. If you absolutely have to have the weight, leave the fish in the net and put the BogaGrip on the net, lift the fish in the net, and then subtract the net weight. You'll have your weight and the fish will be in much better shape. I mostly use them to hold a fish in the water when trying to revive it. It's just a great way to hold a fish if it is a bit worn out after being caught. When the water is warm in the summer, it can take a long time to revive a large muskie, and the BogaGrip is a wonderful tool for that.

I also use a BogaGrip to test my leaders to make sure they are properly built and won't fail when it's go-time. I tie my leader up, check everything twice, and then glue the knots with a touch of superglue. When the glue is dry, take your BogaGrip and put the snap on it, and then pull on it to 35 pounds to make sure that nothing is going to give.

For many reasons the BogaGrip is a great tool to have in your boat bag.
KIP VIETH

Fish-Handling Gloves

I'm a firm believer in wearing fish-handling gloves. It's another tool that gives me a little more comfort when I'm handling fish for the release. Gloves protect your hands from the teeth of the fish and make me a little more comfortable when I have my hands near those razor-sharp teeth. They also protect the fish being handled by reducing the amount of protective slime removed from the fish. Another great benefit is that they give someone new to handling such large fish a better grip and a little more comfort, so they aren't as likely to freak out on a fish that is often the biggest they have ever handled. I highly recommend them when wrangling the beasts.

Bump Board

Everyone wants to know just how big your muskie was. The quickest and best way to measure a fish is on a bump board. The key is to keep the muskie out of the water for as little time as you can. If everything goes as planned, I can unhook, snap a few grip-and-grin photos, and then put the fish on the bump board for a quick measure and then back in the water in less than a minute or two. The bump board is a great tool and helps make getting a good measurement quick and easy.

Landing Net or Other Landing Aid

I am a firm believer in some sort of landing net or aid. I think that it is just easier on the fish. I use it as a way to help the fish rest after it has been fighting. I like the flat-bottom nets for this reason. Fish don't seem to thrash as much in the flat-bottom nets or cradles as they do in a standard net. Once the fish is in the net, I leave the net with the fish in it in the water. I then get everything ready for a quick release while someone holds the net in the water with the fish. I get my tools out, bump board set up, camera turned on, and fish-handling gloves put on. Once everything is ready to go, I'll try to remove the hook while the fish is in the net. Then it's a quick lift out of the water and net, picture taken, and the fish measured and then back into the water. One thing I would recommend is getting a bigger net rather than a smaller one. A bigger net is easier on the fish and gives them a little more breathing room, so they can rest with as little stress as possible.

A high-quality landing aid can ensure that a muskie is released with as little harm as possible.
JON LUKE

FLIES

Opinions on flies are as vast as the selection of flies at most well-stocked fly shops. Every fly angler has their own theories and favorites when it comes to fly selection. We all have our favorite flies and color combinations that seem to work for us. I think it has more to do with the confidence in that particular fly than anything else. If we know that it works, we tend to use it. Muskie fishing is probably more about confidence than any other type of fly fishing. If an angler has caught or moved a bunch of muskies with a certain fly pattern or color combination, that is most often the one they throw. I have always said that if a muskie wants to eat, it'll eat a dirty sock with hooks in it. When the trigger flips, it doesn't matter what the fly looks like or does—they're just going to eat it. Now, can a certain pattern or color trigger a strike? By all means.

The world of muskie fly tying has grown by leaps and bounds. The reason for this is that there just isn't a lot of good commercially tied flies. The reason for this is that the market is relatively small and the cost of shipping and handling such large flies is expensive. The large fly suppliers' margins are just not big enough for them to pursue this space. As the market continues to grow, this will most likely change, and we'll see more and more quality commercially tied flies come to market. This fact is

Pick a fly, any fly.
MIKE DVORAK

responsible for most muskie anglers tying their own flies or buying them from guides and other small suppliers. There are some remarkable tiers out there, and they just keep getting better and better. I'm lucky to have been exposed to some of the best muskie fly tiers in the world here in the Upper Midwest. The Upper Midwest is the epicenter of the muskie on the fly, and we are blessed with some of the best fisheries, anglers, and muskie fly innovators in this very small but growing community.

The evolution of muskie flies has been very cool to watch. The flies I used to fish years ago look nothing like the ones that we are fishing today. We started with basically a great big Deceiver or a large Dahlberg Diver. Now we fish everything from intricately tied, double- and triple-sectioned flies with large profiles to big foam top-water boilers. Today's flies are somewhat of a knock-off of the greats that came before. Names like Blanton, Popovich, and Clouser all paved the way for the innovative muskie flies that have developed over the past few decades. The person that is probably more responsible for many of the styles that are currently being fished is Brad Bohen. He had the creativity and insight to take what the gentlemen before him had done and move it to the next level. Brad's key to success is that he spent hours on the water testing and fine-tuning his flies into fish-catching works of art. He continues to innovate and push the boundaries. Many of us owe a great deal of our success to the path that Brad cut for future guides and anglers.

Most modern fly design is based on Brad's original designs. New fly tiers are tying some truly amazing work. One thing to keep in mind, however, is that it's not how the fly looks, it's how it fishes. I have tied three of the same pattern at the same time, and only one of them really had the magic. Sometimes a fly has to be fished awhile for it to break in. Flies are a funny thing. We all know what we are looking for in a fly, and the more you do it, the pickier you become. There are two basic kinds of muskie flies: topwater flies and subsurface flies. Both categories have their place and ways of fishing.

Gabe Schubert, Jon Luke, and I were fishing together at muskie camp several years ago. I had tied a fly that I was pretty proud of. I had fished it with clients the week before and thought that it might have the mojo that we are always looking for. I pulled it out that day and started fishing it, and had that fly working pretty well. Gabe was fishing in the back of the boat. My fly swam into the boat darting side to side just like I wanted it to. Gabe looked at it and then looked at me and said, "That one has it." Finally, I had the blessing from Muskie Jesus on one of my flies. I still mourn the loss of that fly. It was my first with the blessing.

Gabe, aka Muskie Jesus, spinning up his magic
JON LUKE

Choosing a Fly

There are five things that I look at when I'm choosing a fly. Every fly reacts in a different manner. It's picking up on the fly and how it's behaving that is most important when it comes to fly selection. Once again, experience will tell you if a fly you're working has that certain something. I learned this from Gabe years ago. He could look at one of the flies that I was fishing and tell that it just didn't have it. I would most likely try to steal one of his for the day. Getting one of Gabe's flies is like successfully robbing Fort Knox. He keeps a pretty close eye on them. If you are lucky enough to get one, you guard it with your life. They are that special to our little group that fishes and guides together.

1. Action

This is by far the biggest thing that I look for in a fly that I'm fishing. It mostly applies to the flies that I fish subsurface. Topwater flies are a different game. For topwater flies I just look at how big the fly is and the type of movement it has. It is either a big bang or a subtler diving action. That is basically all there really is for topwater action. Trying to figure out what kind of movement a muskie is looking for in the topwater presentation is the main concern when fishing that type of fly. Are they looking for a truly aggressive presentation with a fast *bang, bang, bang* from a large popper or boiler, or do they want the subtler dive-and-sit that a diver has? Experience will point you in the right direction on this.

With subsurface there are a ton of different flies, with a ton of different actions. Picking the one special fly that you are going to use can be a daunting proposition. I know what works the best for me where I fish. Anglers and guides from other parts of the country might have a different view of what works for them. It's hard to sit here in the Upper Midwest and tell you what action works best in Tennessee. Some guys like the Game Changer flies and some like the Buford type, while others have a totally different view of what works. In another three years who knows what kind of flies will be available. So, look for a fly with the action that seems right for your situation and that *you* are confident with. Confidence is the biggest factor. If you're not confident in that fly, take it off. You're not going to fish it with the right amount of zeal. If you don't feel it, it will have a negative effect on your fishing. I tell clients to let me know if they aren't feeling the fly. I think that a lot of clients feel that if I picked it out, it must work. I'd rather have you fishing something that you're confident with than something you think I want you to fish.

2. Speed

A lot of factors come into play when considering speed and fly choice, including time of year, water temperatures, wind conditions, and depth of the fly. The warmer the water, usually the faster a fly can be worked. I'm not a big "speed kills" guy. I usually tell my clients to slow it down more than speed it up. That being said, eight out of ten times I'm fishing when the water temperatures are in the 33- to 50-degree range. Muskies are cold-blooded animals, and with colder water comes slower metabolisms. I call it "slow and low." Even in the summer I still probably strip a lot slower than most people. I want that subsurface fly to look like a baitfish that is holding on for dear life—in other words, a very easy meal.

If I do fish muskies in the warmer summer months, I like to throw a topwater presentation. When the water gets above 70 degrees, I will bang a big boiler or popper up top. I run that popper very aggressively, making a ton of noise and looking to wake up a big one.

Picking a fly that is going to move at the right speed for your situation is an important factor to consider. If I'm going to work a subsurface fly faster, I most likely will use one with a slenderer profile. If I'm going low and slow, I want one with a bigger profile. Same with topwater. If I'm fishing aggressively, I will go with a big boiler type. If I want to fish a topwater slower, I mostly fish big diver-type flies. It's not that complicated, and I will get into more detail on fly action in the following chapter.

3. Depth/Casting

Where in the water column do you want to be fishing? Of course, fly selection can have a big impact on this factor. You wouldn't throw a big foam blockhead on if you're looking to get your fly down. It's really just common sense. A lot has to do

THE FLY YOU PICK IN THE
FALL MAY DIFFER FROM
THE ONE YOU USE IN THE
SUMMER SEASON.

JON LUKE

with what kind of fly line you are throwing. Is it a floating line or a sinking line? If it is a sinking line, what is the sink rate? Is there a lot of current or wind? These are just a few of the factors to consider when trying to figure out what depth your fly will be working.

A good portion of the muskie flies out there have a lot of bucktail in them. This can be a pretty buoyant material. If you're trying to get that fly down, you'll need to have a pretty good sinking line. I'm not a big fan of adding weight to my flies or leaders. Remember point number one? I feel it takes a lot of the action out of the fly. In my opinion, it makes the fly look unnatural. I believe in controlling the depth of the fly with your fly line, speed of retrieve, and proper fly selection. Test the fly you want to fish and see if it is getting where you want it to be. If it isn't, adjust one of the factors to get it in front of a muskie's face.

Your casting skills and your setup will also be factors in choosing a fly. If you're not comfortable casting a larger fly, you'll have to downsize your fly. I'd rather a client cast a smaller fly than be uncomfortable all day casting a larger one. A happy caster is usually a happy angler. If you dread making the next cast because you're afraid to, you're just not going to do a good job fishing. Cast what you're comfortable with.

Your equipment is also going to be a factor. Let's say that you are just getting into muskie fishing with a fly rod. The only rod that you currently have that might work is a 9-weight. You rig it up and are all set to give it a try. Now, you aren't going to throw an 18-inch double Musky Rat with that rod, and if you do, it won't be for long. Pick the right fly that your setup can handle. That's why I always preach using a size or two bigger in your setup than you think you should. Like I said earlier, you can't throw a 15-inch muskie fly on a 3-weight rod, but you can throw a size 14 fly on a 10-weight.

4. Season and Food Source

What fly you pick can also depend on what season you're in. I'm not going to roll up in November when the water temperature is 34 degrees with a topwater presentation. Some folks also will run smaller flies in the early part of the season, believing that most of the bait is small so they'll run a smaller fly. If I'm fishing one of our lakes with a large population of northern ciscoes (or, as they are known here in Minnesota, tullibees) in the fall, I'm throwing a large white fly. They spawn on large rock humps when the water temperature hits around 40 degrees. It's a key time to be fishing, and the fly has to have a white coloration to it.

Knowing what the fish are looking for is very helpful. If the body of water has a lot of perch, I go with the fire tiger color in a medium size. If I'm on a river and know that there are a lot of redhorse suckers, I'm throwing a large brown with a little pink hue in it. So, knowing what a fish is eating in a particular part of the season and how active they are will help dictate your fly selection. It's like what we talked about previously: Knowing what is going on around you and the waters you are fishing always makes your decisions easier.

Here in the Upper Midwest rivers, redhorse suckers are the muskies' number one target. In the lakes they can have many baitfish to consider, but I always look for the T-bone steak that is swimming in the lake. I want to imitate the fattest, richest bait there is. Most of the time that is some kind of whitefish, cisco, or sucker. Perch can be a close second. A muskie will eat almost anything if given the opportunity, yet these rich and tasty baitfish hold a special place in their heart. A lot of my flies will try to match that baitfish. It can be a silver/white pattern to try to match a cisco or whitefish, or a bronze or brownish natural to match the suckers. I usually start with this type of color scheme and work from there. I also have plenty of other color schemes—pinks, fire tiger, chartreuse, and a lot of other combos. On any given day, any of them can be the color. Once again, it comes down to confidence and what you have had past success with or what jumps out at you.

5. Finishing

How does the fly finish? During the summer months, about 80 percent of muskies eat on a figure eight or right at the side of the boat. If the fly you are using can't be manipulated boatside by the angler, you are going to be fighting an uphill battle. A fly stalling as you run your figure eight can send a muskie heading for the depths. You need your fly to be lifelike all the way through your cast, and that includes boatside. If your fly is too big and you can't keep it turning on the figure eight, you have a problem. It the fly is too small and does nothing, that can be a problem too. It's finding the right balance and making sure that your fly is as effective at 40 feet out as it is at your rod tip.

Topwater Flies

Topwater is basically just that: something that floats on top of the water and is most likely some kind of popper or diver-type fly. When muskie fly fishing first started to get a grip on fly anglers, many of us started fishing a lot of topwater presentations. Most of this was by pure accident. I would be fishing smallmouths and throw a diver up near a logjam, give it a good dive, and watch as a 40-inch muskie blew the thing right out of the water. Twelve dollars later and no fish, and I'd think, "Man, that would be pretty cool if we could actually land one of those things." So, the quest began. That's the story for a lot of us that caught the muskie bug. We'd see them while fishing for other species and just had to try to land one. Topwater seemed like the logical solution. We had seen and lost a few fish while smallmouth fishing using topwater flies, so we charged forward. We would buy the biggest divers we could find, add a little wire leader, and the game was on.

Just like all muskie fly patterns, they evolved and now you have some really cool topwater flies. I've seen huge boilers and poppers, big divers, small ducks, and large frogs. Just like everything in muskie fly fishing, things will continue to evolve, and topwater flies will do the same. It should be interesting.

This old-school boiler was one of the first big topwater flies I can remember casting.
KIP VIETH

A diver sometimes has the presentation a muskie is looking for.
KIP VIETH

A big blockhead is the perfect fly to move a bunch of water and often triggers a strike. The articulated hook increases the hookup rate.
KIP VIETH

There is nothing like a huge fish blowing up a top-water fly. It is simply a pure adrenaline rush. The one drawback to the topwater game is the hookup rate. It is extremely low and can be very frustrating at times. The wow factor is the first thing that can go wrong. When a big fish eats a topwater presentation, it is often such a surprise that the hook-set is usually early or not at all. We are often so surprised by it that we lift the rod like we're trout fishing, or we simply stare in amazement as the fish swims away. I'm guilty of both, and if you do it long enough you will be to, so get used to it.

The other and probably the biggest thing going against the topwater angler is the bite factor. Think of a muskie as an alligator. The clamping force of an alligator is something like 2,000 psi (pounds per square inch). If they bite something, it's not moving. A muskie is the same way. I'm not saying their bite is 2,000 psi, but it is substantial. Most modern-day topwater flies for muskies are made out of some kind of foam or at least have a good amount of foam in them. When a muskie eats something, it's not going to let it go. It's trying to crush and kill it. Let's take a closer look at your big foam boiler. A muskie eats it and sinks its rather large teeth into that big foam head. You react perfectly—you let the fish turn away, get tight, and strip-set with a vengeance. The fly does absolutely nothing. That big foam head is clamped into the muskie's mouth, and no matter how hard you strip-set that fly isn't going anywhere. The fish's clamping force is not going to allow that fly to move. The only time it is going to move is when the fish realizes that it is a foam boiler and spits it out at you. You go from adrenaline and excitement to disappointment and frustration in just a matter of seconds. Just be prepared and know that this is part of the topwater game and can be very painful at times. That is why smallmouth bass also hold a special spot in my heart. They simply love to eat topwater presentations and do it willingly. They also don't have a jaw made of steel or clamp down like a gator.

When a muskie blows up a topwater fly, it is magical and worth all the suffering that you might have experienced. Just keep in mind that like trout, 98 percent of a muskie's diet is under the surface of the water. Baitfish are king in its diet. That being said, nothing beats a huge fish eating a topwater presentation. It can be like no other fishing experience that you have ever had in your life.

Subsurface Flies

This type of fly is what the majority of muskie fly anglers use on a day-to-day basis. A muskie's diet consists of baitfish about 98 percent of the time. Subsurface flies have evolved the most, and their designs continue to do so. You have to keep in mind that muskie fishing is still in an experimental stage—flies especially. New materials and techniques continue to come down the pipeline in an ever-growing quest to find that perfect muskie fly.

Most modern subsurface flies are designed to push a lot of water underneath the surface, while having a fair amount of flash and sparkle to attract fish. The most important factor, in my opinion, is the movement of the fly. I feel this is the main factor in triggering a muskie to eat a fly. It isn't how the fly looks, it's how it moves. Most muskie anglers know what they are looking for, and fly design has evolved with the introduction of new higher-tech materials and techniques to create some flies that really move beautifully. These materials have made it possible to come up with great flies, and it is exciting to think of the flies that will come in the future.

Some Favorite Muskie Flies
Buford

A Buford-style fly getting it done
MIKE DVORAK

Game Changer

The Game Changer has been a game changer with its unique movement and innovations.
FLYMEN COMPANY

El Chupacabra

Sometimes a smaller fly is what the doctor ordered. The El Chupacabra by Nick Granato is often the perfect answer.
KIP VIETH

Wildwood's Mynard Skynard

Wildwood's Mynard Skynard combines the best of the T-Bone, Buford, and Game Changer. Moving a lot of water without much bulk was the desired effect of the fly.

KIP VIETH

Luke's Musky Rat

Jon Luke was always thinking ahead of the curve. He was one of the first to come up with curly tails on flies to give them more action and enticement, as seen here on his **Musky Rat**.

JON LUKE

Kip Notes

- Put time in on the water.
- Buy and use the best equipment possible. Don't skimp. Muskies have a way of finding the weakest links and exposing them.
- Find what works best for you. Cast a lot of rods and lines. Figure it out.
- Use what gives you the best chance of being successful. It's not just about the rods and lines either—remember the sunglasses.
- Keep your hooks sharp!
- Learn your knots and become good at tying them.
- Fish the flies that you have confidence in, and fish the heck out of them.
- Confidence, confidence, confidence.

CHAPTER FIVE

CASTING AND RETRIEVING

Nothing about fly fishing for muskies is easy, and nothing makes that more evident than casting and retrieving a large muskie fly for eight hours. It's both a physical and a mental strain. If you're not in the right physical and mental shape, it can be a torturous process at best. There is nothing pretty about it.

TEN WAYS TO IMPROVE YOUR CASTING

If you think that your FFF casting class is going to help, you're barking up the wrong tree. Most dyed-in-the-wool casting instructors would cringe at the way that I teach people how to throw a large fly. If you were observant, you would see that I used the word *throw*, not *cast*, in the last sentence. Yes, it's still casting, but when you're trying to heave half a chicken through the air, the art of casting is somewhat lost. The plain and simple truth is the less you aerialize the line, the better. You also have to keep in mind that casting something that big is hard. You don't want any wasted motion if possible. Making four false casts every time you make a cast will kick your butt. It may even leave you in the fetal position in the bottom of the boat, begging for mercy. You'd be surprised at the number of clients that have cried uncle with a lot of the day left to go.

Learning a few tricks of the trade, so to speak, can go a long way toward making sure that you remain in the game. You do not want to be put on the disabled list with two days to go on your muskie trip. Remember, casting large muskie flies is like no other type of fly casting. You may have thrown a 12-weight for tarpon in the Florida

With proper preparation, it's possible to cast large muskie flies.

NATE SIPPLE

Keys or chased peacocks in the Amazon rain forest, but even that is not close to what it takes to throw a large muskie fly. It is probably unlike anything you have experienced. The sooner you forget about a standard cast or what you think it will be like, the better. It's simply a whole new world if you haven't experienced it. The fewer preconceived notions that you have coming into it, the better.

Here are ten things that you can do to make your casting better and more efficient:

1. Practice

There is nothing more important than practice in any sport that you participate in. If you want to become good at casting, practice is key. This is probably the most overlooked exercise in all of fly fishing. If anglers just practiced a little, their success on the water would increase substantially.

Each trip usually involves a drive to the water. This is the time when if the client is new, we small-talk and the topic usually comes up of how long they have been fly fishing. I had one client tell me that he had been fishing for thirty years. In the back of my mind I'm thinking great, this should be a pretty good day. Nothing could have been further from the truth. The client just simply couldn't cast. I have found this to be common in a lot of our trips. We get a fair number of beginners or clients that haven't fished much for larger warmwater species. Casting is key to success when fishing for these species.

After watching this client struggle mightily, I asked him where he had fished in those thirty years. He informed me that he and his fishing partner had done a big four-day trip every year throughout North America. I then asked if he fished locally where he lived at all. He said no, he just did the big trip every year. The light went on with that statement and I immediately did the math: $4 \times 30 = 120$. So he had a total of 120 days of fly-fishing experience with no other practice. He had basically been fly fishing for a total of four months, not thirty years. The other thing that jumped out was that if you're only casting for four days once a year, there is no way to build up any muscle memory. It was almost like he was starting from scratch every year. The client was a wonderful guy and we did catch a few fish, but if he would have just practiced and had a little more experience, his trip would have been twice the success that it was.

Vince Lombardi said, "Practice does not make perfect. Only perfect practice makes perfect." Growing up in Wisconsin, I thought it only fitting to throw a Coach Lombardi quote in there. That quote is right on. Just as I spoke about actually fishing the equipment that you're thinking about buying, you need to practice where you are going to fish. That is on the water. Fishing is not the time to practice. Practice is the time to practice. They should be two entirely different things. If you think you are going to go fishing and figure a few things out, you are most likely setting yourself up for disappointment. I'm not saying that you shouldn't work on things while you're fishing, but it shouldn't be the big things. Things to work on during fishing are better figure eights, working your fly, and fine-tuning your cast. It shouldn't be learning how to open up your cast, water load, or double haul. These are all big-picture items and are best learned during a quality practice casting session.

A quality practice is not in your backyard or a field at the local park—it is on the water! You can't get the true feel of a cast and how your rod and system work in a field somewhere. It doesn't have to be much, just some kind water. It can be a small pond, a dock on a lake, from a boat, or even a pool. Any type of water will do. The great thing about practicing on the water is that you can get the full effect of a fishing experience. You can practice all the aspects of your fishing. Not only can you work on your cast, but you can also practice working the fly, figure eights, keeping the line tight, and even getting the feel of the strip-set. These are all things that are crucial to success while muskie fishing. Being able to work on every part of your game is beneficial and you'll be glad you did. You don't see a sports team just practicing one aspect of the game—they practice all aspects of the game in every possible situation. Practice casting in all situations, and that includes the wind. Now, if a lawn or field is all you have access to, I guess I'll take that over not practicing at all. Every little bit helps.

2. Get in Casting Shape

No one will ever accuse me of being in shape. I haven't been in shape since the second grade, but I am in pretty decent casting shape. Anyone can achieve casting shape. If you're doing the proper amount of practicing, chances are you'll be in pretty good casting shape. Everything usually hurts a little after a day of casting to muskies. It's just the nature of the beast. There is no way around it, at least for us old folks. Pain meds and anti-inflammatories are a staple at most muskie camps. That being said, there are things you can do to make sure it's just aches and pains and not something that can really put you out of commission.

The biggest thing that I see is either tennis or golfer's elbow. If you have fly casted long and hard enough, you have most likely experienced this in the past. It can be painful and annoying when you're trying to fish. I used to suffer from it, and still will get a flare-up every now and again. I don't fish like I used to either. I'm too busy rowing a boat to actually fish anymore. The best thing for it is rest, but when you're on a three-day muskie trip, that really isn't an option. What you need to do is get your arm/elbow in shape before you go on your trip. There are a lot of exercises and tools out there to get that part of the arm in shape. The best one I've found is some kind of squeezing device that helps stretch and strengthen the muscles and tendons in and around the elbow. I've even used a tennis ball at times. While sitting watching TV, just use one of these devices a bit each day for a couple of weeks and it will go a long way in making sure your elbow doesn't fail you.

The shoulder is the other weak link in a caster's body. If your joint goes, you're pretty much out of commission for a long time. The elbow can usually be dealt with by pain meds, braces, etc., but the shoulder is a different story. Getting it warmed up goes a long way in ensuring it doesn't cause problems. There are plenty of shoulder exercises that you can do to help strengthen the joint as well. A simple Google search will provide more than enough to get you started. Proper casting techniques can also help avoid problems down the road. We'll touch on this a bit more later in the chapter. A little preventive medicine can go a long way in keeping you in the game.

The other thing I see a lot, especially in the fall, is that an angler's hands start to break down. In the cold and wet, they can crack and become a real distraction. At the end of the season, my hands look like someone took a cheese grater to them. The first thing that I recommend is a stripping guard. It protects your finger from the wear and tear of stripping the fly in. Every cast has to be stripped in all the way to the boat and worked. If your stripping finger is all beat up, you don't finish a lot of your casts, and when it comes time to strip-set, I don't want to see you wince in pain as you try to strip-set on a fish of a lifetime. It's a $2 item and can mean the difference between a fish in the net or a blown opportunity.

The second thing is to drink a lot of water. I am guilty of not doing this enough in the fall. In the summer I'm very conscious of it due to the heat. I try to drink a ton of water during those dog days of summer. In the fall when the temperatures cool down, I'm just not drinking enough. It can really help keep your skin from becoming an issue. You should also moisturize your hands well at the end of the day. There are many really good hand treatments out there. Apply them generously and keep it up throughout the season.

Keeping your body in shape is key. It's the most important tool that you have for muskie fishing. If you don't pay attention to it, it can fail just like any other tool.

Wearing a stripping finger guard can help land a fish.
KIP VIETH

3. Use the Right Setup

Now, we talked a lot already in the previous chapter about setups for chasing musk-ies. We won't go into much detail here since we covered most of it—I just want to reiterate how important the right setup is for your style and the waters that you fish. If it doesn't match your style and the way that you like to fish, you'll get frustrated and possibly hurt yourself. If you are overworking because your setup is wrong, it can mess up your elbow and shoulder pretty quickly. But the biggest thing that it might mess with is your head. If you're struggling to cast and things are getting painful, your head is most likely not in it. When you lose your confidence and doubt creeps in, you've lost. When that happens, that is when a muskie will show up and you just won't be there to take advantage of it. Having the proper setup goes a long way in eliminating the mental fatigue factor.

Styles also change as you evolve in the sport. The rods that I thought were the best thing going a few years back rarely see the outside of their rod tubes these days. I have just grown into a different type of muskie angler and guide than I was ten years ago.

I throw different lines and flies and fish different casts than I used to. I have become a much more disciplined angler and guide, and my equipment has changed with that discipline and experience. Don't be surprised when this happens to you. The only constant in muskie fly fishing is change. Everything is different from year to year or even day to day. One thing is for certain: You will evolve and with that so will your equipment. Experience is the great teacher.

4. Remember, You're Not Pete Kutzer

If you've watched any of the Orvis casting videos, you know who Pete Kutzer is. If you haven't, I recommend you do so. I'll watch Pete's videos every now and again and still manage to learn something. Pete is Orvis's main casting instructor and the host of most of their casting videos. I hate to be the bearer of bad news, but you're not him, and the odds that you can cast like him aren't good. I've fished with Pete many times. To say that it is humbling to watch him cast would be an understatement. I thought I was a decent caster—not great mind you, but I can get the job done nine out of ten times. When I fish with Pete, I realize that I have a long way to go.

Pete Kutzer with a well-earned muskie
GABE SCHUBERT

Now, I've seen Pete cast a 15-inch muskie fly 80 feet and it is impressive. We'll get into why that's not necessarily a good thing a little later. That being said, there are only a handful of casters that can pull that off on a standard overhead cast. Chances of me pulling that cast off without pulling a major muscle or driving a 6/0 muskie fly somewhere into my body are slim to none. The sooner you realize that, the better off you'll be. If you have a vision of using those skills that an FFF casting instructor taught you, I would think again.

Muskie casting isn't pretty. It is blue-collar fishing at its finest. It's all about getting the job done, and it usually isn't glamorous. Think of Mike Rowe's TV show *Dirty Jobs* meets fly fishing. You won't be casting 50 feet with a supertight loop. Get the visions of the latest Orvis catalog where the angler is casting a tight loop 75 feet out of your head. It's not realistic.

Why isn't it realistic? There are several factors at play. The first one is the size of the flies that we throw. They can range anywhere from 6 inches all the way up to 20 inches in some cases. The wind resistance and mass of the fly aren't conducive to making tight loops. The physics of the cast make throwing these large flies difficult. The second factor is the sinking line that you are throwing. Along with the fly having a lot of mass, the fly line does also. Getting all of that weight to turn over tightly is a challenge. The third factor is the fact that you're bringing all that fly line in. If you're fishing correctly, you're stripping that line all the way into the guides and turning your fly on a figure eight on every cast. Getting all that line back out and started with a bunch of false casts just isn't very efficient. If you are doing more than two false casts per cast, you're false casting way too much.

It's all about efficiencies. Aerializing your fly line while muskie fishing just isn't a good idea. Less is more. The more false casting you do, the more stuff can go wrong and the harder it is on your body. If you plan on fishing for more than a day, you'll need to cast with very few false casts. Saltwater anglers and even my smallmouth clients can afford to pick up their cast with 30 feet of fly line outside of their rod tip. When you do this, you are generating a ton of line speed on the first cast, thus getting a tight loop right away. If you pick up your line early muskie fishing, you'll be missing a vital part of your fishing. Sooner or later that early pickup will cost you a fish. Every cast needs to be worked till the end, and that includes turning the fly on a figure eight each time. If you're working each cast correctly, the figure eight can also get tiresome. That is another reason you need to be efficient with every cast. The more your line is in the air and not on the water, the more that can go wrong in muskie fishing—not just with the cast, but with everything. I call it the trickle-down effect. When your cast isn't efficient, it affects everything.

Say you are floating down a river in a drift boat, casting to the structure that presents itself. Your cast didn't go where you wanted it to go, so you pick up and cast again. Much to your amazement, the cast went to the same spot that it did the first time. This brings us to an important rule: Fish everything out no matter where it ends up. You should have just fished the first cast. It's muskie fishing and you never know. You now are on the second cast and you finally decide to fish it. The logjam you were trying to fish with the first cast is slowly drifting by and you are now feeling rushed.

Work every cast as if the next world record is going to be caught.
JON LUKE

You bring the fly in and do a poor job on the figure eight. You now start your third cast to the same spot, trying to get to the logjam that is now behind you. It takes you five false casts to get to your spot. Your elbow feels a slight twinge in it as you unload the cast. You work the fly back, and as the fly comes around the wood, a muskie swims out from its haunt and eats. The fly and fish are coming downriver toward you. You grab the fly line and start stripping as fast as you can, but the line never comes really tight. Your elbow is now screaming in pain from the frantic stripping. The fish looks up at you with that sneer that only muskies have and spits the fly out. As he swims back to the logjam you can almost hear him say, "Nice try, knucklehead." Now repeat this scenario several times throughout the day except for the part about the muskie eating, and you can see how one wrong inefficient cast can cause all kinds of problems. It all started with one cast not going where you wanted it to go and went downhill from there. Remember, it's hard to catch a fish when your fly isn't in the water. That is the other thing about casting efficiency: It leads to good fishing efficacy, which leads to more opportunities for the fish to see and react to your fly.

Here's how it should have went: You make a cast to a logjam but leave it about 10 feet short of the target. Since you missed your target, you let the fly sink a little. You begin working the fly back to the boat. Out of the corner of your eye, you see a large shadow slowly get behind your fly. You keep working the fly all the way to the boat. As you get the fly closer, you reach out with the rod and the fly. You begin moving the fly away from the boat, diverting the fish's attention back to the fly. As you stick your fly rod down into the water, pushing the fly deeper, and begin your figure eight, the fish charges the fly. He smashes it, going away from you and the boat. A simple hard strip-set with an already tight line, and the fish is hooked and landed.

That is the perfect scenario and seldom does it happen that way. You can, however, see the difference in the whole smoothness of the second scenario. There wasn't any frantic casting or movements. You just went about your business and fished the situation that you were given. There was a heck of a lot less energy expended in the second scenario than the first. This leads to a more enjoyable day on the water and usually a more productive one. You avoided the trickle-down effect, or as one client put it, the snowball effect. When it starts going bad, it usually doesn't get better. Slow down, take a deep breath, and just fish. Haste makes waste, especially when muskie fishing with fly rods. Years ago I had a client who also guided a bit tell me that if the cast feels bad from the start, just stop and start over because it most likely isn't going to get any better. It's all about being efficient, not pretty.

Keeping everything tight leads to more landed fish.
JON LUKE

5. Keep It Tight

One of the hardest things about writing about casting is trying to describe what is going on. I've found it difficult to transfer my teaching style into words. I'll do my best. When I say keep it tight, it means keep as much slack out of the fly line as possible. This goes against the standard fly-casting mentality. What we are trying to do is keep the shock out of the system. We want to keep the casting as smooth as possible. You're probably thinking about a silky cast, like the kind you see at the Fly Fishing Film Tour. Get that image out of your head. We talked about efficiency in the previous section. Now, I must have you totally confused. Let's talk about the standard cast. We are taught by most casting instructors, including me, that we want to start a forward cast just before the fly straightens out on the backcast. This is great when you are throwing small trout flies. The problem with that cast when it comes to large flies is that you're introducing shock into the system.

As you can see in the photo on the next page, the angler is bringing the fly forward just as the line is about to straighten out. If that fly is a muskie fly and I bring it forward and the line isn't tight, that slack will introduce shock into the system. When flies are that big and you bring them forward, that shock will cause your cast to jump. You have to remember that when you throw large flies, that loop behind you is going to be a lot bigger than a loop you might throw with a size 14 Adams. With the bigger loop from the bigger fly, you are now introducing a bigger shock into your casting stroke. This will make the rod thump, and if the thump is big enough, it may even cause the rod to break. We want to have constant tension on the rod and not a shock. We want the rod to load as gently and as consistently as it can with such large flies.

You want to bring your line forward when the backcast is straight back. This will take that slack or shock out the system and provide for a smoother transition into the forward cast. You should feel the rod tug back just before you bring it forward for the forward cast. There is a ton of mass going behind you, and when it straightens out, you will feel the rod thump. That thump will let you know to begin your forward cast.

By taking the shock out of the system, you are also taking the shock out of every-thing else that is involved in the cast. Probably the biggest thing you're helping is the fly line. Muskie fishing is notoriously hard on fly lines. The stress they are under is incredible. Fly lines weren't made to take this kind of shock for extended periods of time. The shock of constantly casting large flies will break down a fly line. Imagine that someone keeps pulling on the end of your arm with short, powerful thrusts over and over and over again. After a while something is going to give. That is what is happening to your fly line. Sooner or later it's going to crack. It's not a matter of if, but when. Lines have been getting better and better, and they hold up a lot better than they did just a few years ago. Line manufacturers understand what is taking place in the world of muskie fly fishing and are designing very sophisticated lines for the application. This is why taking the shock out of the system is important.

Jared Ehlers opening it up and sending it
JON LUKE

Another part of the system is you. Taking the shock out of the line helps the caster as well. The stress on the elbow, shoulder, and hand is drastically reduced with a more fluid transition from the backcast to the forward cast. You are reducing the shock to your casting hand. It might not seem like much, but if you're on the water grinding for four days, every little bit helps. The other thing that we don't like to talk much about is the fly itself. No one wants to think about a 5/0 muskie fly finding its way into someone's back or head. The thought of that would make anyone cringe. I've only experienced it once in a client's finger, and I don't need to do it again. Keeping everything tight makes this a heck of a lot less likely to happen.

Tight is right. The more you keep everything tight, the better off all your fishing will be. The only time that you need to experience any shock and awe is when the muskie you have been chasing for three years decides to eat. If everything is tight, the chances of landing it go way up.

6. Open It Up

To cast these large flies, you also need to open up your cast a bit. As we discussed, we're trying to eliminate the shock on the fly line. The best way to do this is to open up your cast. What we mean when we say to open it up is to give it a bigger loop. The best way to do this is to go to an oval or Belgium cast. When the wind blows and the big wind-resistant flies start getting pushed around a bit, using this cast can be a game changer. Pete does a great job of explaining this in one of his videos on casting large flies. Here is the link: https://www.youtube.com/watch?v=7v3J5xHIJOk.

By opening the cast up, you are keeping constant tension on the line and not shocking it. There is no stopping the rod at 10 and 2 o'clock. You keep the rod moving toward its target. It is a very smooth cast. Casting like this, you'll be able to fish for multiple days and not suffer as much fatigue. If you are going to fish with the standard-type cast, this is by far the most efficient and effective way of doing it.

7. Keep It Short

Pete loaded up the rod and banged out a 70-foot cast like it was nothing. I sat there in the rower's seat amazed at how easily he did it. After the shock wore off, I looked at him and asked why the heck he was casting so far. His answer was typical Pete: "'Cause it's fun and I can." My reply was probably not what he wanted to hear, but I informed him that muskie casting that far is stupid. If a muskie ate your fly way out there, you would never get a hook stuck in it. Muskie fly fishing is a close-combat affair.

I would say the perfect cast is about 40 to 50 feet. Much more than that, and it gets really hard to strip-set the hook into a muskie's hard mouth. There is just too much distance between you and the fish. Fly lines do stretch, but not enough to be a factor. The biggest factor for the fly angler is line management. If you are fishing at those distances, there is most likely going to be substantial slack/bow in the line. Slack is probably the biggest factor there is when it comes to not putting a fish in the net. Not coming tight to the fish and getting a quality hook-set is the biggest mistake that I see day in and day out on my trips. Over and over again I see clients just not strip-setting like they need to. The tighter the line is, the better things usually work out. You can sometimes get away with a lackluster strip-set if the line is tight to begin with. When a fish eats, you'll need to take up all that slack and get the line tight so that you can perform a proper strip-strike.

When you are fishing at closer ranges, these problems are kept to a minimum. Everything is better when slack is minimal when muskie fly fishing. Keeping it short is simply one of the best practices to get into. Line management is key to taking advantage of any muskie that eats your fly. Tight is right, and the sooner you start getting into that practice, the better off you'll be. Muskies, as I've said, are very unforgiving. Don't give them any reason to not feel the point of your hook.

The other positive about fishing close is you're not trying to kill yourself making long casts. By keeping it short, you're more likely to be in the game longer. If you're not fishing, you're not catching. Staying in the game is key. The positives outweigh the negatives when it comes to fishing close.

Yes, there are some disadvantages to not casting as far. You just aren't covering as much water as you possibly could with a longer cast. The longer the fly is in the water, the better. The benefits of the longer cast are, however, outweighed by keeping the line tight. There's always a tradeoff, but keeping the line tight is by far a bigger advantage than covering more water.

8. Learn How to Haul

We are always looking for an easier way to cast those large muskie flies. One of the best things an angler can do is learn two relatively easy things. The first one is how to single and double haul. It is an important arrow to have in your quiver, and I use it in every part of my fly fishing. From trout to muskie, a double haul or even a single haul can really be the thing that is needed to get the job done. A haul is simply pulling the fly line as the rod loads to increase your line speed. With increased line speed you are also going to tighten your loop, cast in windy conditions better, increase your accuracy, and probably most importantly, decrease the strain on your wrist. Peter Kutzer uses the analogy of a turbo kicking in on a car at the right time. A haul is the same thing. When you apply the haul, you are bending the rod a little more. This bend adds more stored energy to the rod. When you cast, that stored energy is transferred to the cast. The increase of energy is what increases your line speed and tightens your loop.

I usually only add one haul to my muskie casts. I try not to do more than one or two false casts, which we talked about earlier. This brings us to the second trick to help cast large flies. Remember we talked about keeping everything tight on your cast. One of the easiest ways to do this is by using the water to tighten your cast up. We simply call this a water haul. Spey casters have been using this for as long as it has been around. They use the water to load their rods instead of the line weight. It's a simple concept. When using very large flies, I find it a game changer. I can simply apply a slight water haul and shoot my fly easily 50 feet without much of an effort. It's a very fluid act once you get it dialed in. You can come right out of a figure eight, flip the fly back 20 feet or so, let it touch the water briefly, and then fire the forward cast. With the water bending the rod and a slight haul, there is more than enough energy generated to fire a cast a distance of about 50 feet easily. I always said I can teach someone to muskie cast a heck of a lot easier than a regular casting situation.

9. Two-Hand It / Touch and Go

We touched on the use of two-handed Spey rods in the equipment and rigging chapter. They have been around for centuries and are really nothing new. The way that they are being adapted to different fishing situations is what has changed and evolved in the last decade or so. It is no secret that Spey rods have taken fly fishing by storm in the last couple decades. We now have everything from micro Spey rods for small-stream trout to larger specialized rods for muskies. The growth in this segment of fly fishing has been nothing short of amazing, and with that growth has come more and more advances. Equipment and materials just keep getting better and better. With these advances the barriers to this type of fishing are becoming less and less.

If you are looking for a bit of an advantage in your casting, the two-handed cast might be the answer. It's not for everyone, but I see more and more anglers incorporating this type of casting style into their muskie fishing. More rods are coming out that are a blend of Spey and standard rods. Think of a switch rod for muskies, as a standard Spey rod really doesn't have the backbone that is needed for muskies. Rod makers are blending the best of the standard rods and adding a little Spey-type feel to them. They now have a bigger butt section for increased effectiveness when two-handed casting and turning the rod on figure eights. These hybrid rods make water hauling, which we discussed earlier, very easy. I believe the increased power in these rods and the newer design will be the future of the muskie-on-the-fly game. The newer rod technology and techniques are sure to make casting easier.

10. Practice

I was talking to Pete Kutzer about this section before I wrote it. You'll notice that practice is listed as both number 1 and 10: This was Pete's idea. He and I both feel this strongly about practicing your casting. Pete has come to muskie camp several times and helped run the Orvis Muskie School with me. He knows what a challenge muskie fishing is. When he said, "List it twice," I couldn't have agreed more. He also made a point to say that the practice should be on water. When someone that can cast as good as Pete tells you how important practice is, I think we should all listen.

As I was thinking about practice, a story popped into my head that I have told several times. It drives home the point that everyone needs time on the water and how important that is. It also proves the point that fishing should be fun, and you should be able to laugh at yourself. If you can't laugh while muskie fishing, you'll be in a very bad place. I live by what Joe Maddon, former manager of the Chicago Cubs, once said: "Try not to suck." Most of us suck when it comes to muskie fishing—it's just the nature of the game. I have seen some of the best anglers I know blow it muskie

Wisdom of the young: Truman with his first muskie on the fly

JON LUKE

fishing. It's amazing how these fish can bring out the worst in us. I just try to suck a little less each time out. The more you practice, the less you'll suck.

I was fishing with my son and my dear friend Jon Luke a few years back. We were on our annual muskie camp weekend, which we hold every October somewhere in northern Minnesota. It has grown into a pretty cool tradition and gives me a chance to fish a bit, which I rarely do anymore because of my busy guiding schedule. I was rowing as I do most of the time (which to be honest with you, I don't mind). The middle seat of a drift boat is my happy place. Jon finally offered to row for a bit as we slowly drifted down the river. Now, my son never fishes in the front of the boat. The back seat is his spot, and I think it's because he doesn't like me telling him what to do. It's hard to not be somewhat of a guide when it's all you really do. He's grown up to be a pretty good caster and muskie fisherman, though he doesn't take it too seriously. I offered him the front and he refused, so I had no choice but to take it. I stepped up, grabbed my rod, and started casting.

This was probably the first time I had actually tried to muskie fish since the previous year's muskie camp. The problem with the front seat is that everyone on the boat can see what's going on with you. Well, things weren't going too well. I've always struggled a bit casting giant flies, and I'm not afraid to admit it. As I say a lot in this book, muskie fishing isn't easy. I also learned why my son likes the back. I made about fifteen casts and maybe hit my target five times. On the other casts I had fly line everywhere—wrapped around the boat, my feet, and maybe even my head. Finally, my son spoke up and informed me, "Man, your casting sucks." I couldn't really argue with the little punk. Jon looked up and asked me, "What kind of shit show are you running up there? I thought you were this big guide of the year," in a way that only Jon could ask. We were all laughing our butts off when it hit me. I yelled back at them, "Hey you jerks, I don't get to fish anymore—I'm too busy rowing a boat!" I have been fly fishing for over thirty-five years and it's not like riding a bike. Muskie fly fishing is something that needs to be practiced. It's a totally different game than most types of fly fishing. You need to practice the craft on the water to really be proficient at it. Trust me, I know.

TEN TIPS TO HELP YOU WORK YOUR FLY PROPERLY

To me, this is perhaps the biggest factor in trying to make a muskie eat, and it is the one thing that is somewhat in the angler's control. We touched briefly on fly types and color combos in the previous chapter, but none of those factors are as important as working the fly properly. This is the one thing that you can do to help trigger a strike. There are as many opinions on how to work a muskie fly as there are shades of green in a Minnesota forest in the summer. We have talked at length about a muskie only eating when it really wants to. If a muskie is following your fly, it is at least a little bit interested. It might just be curious, but at least it's looking at your presentation. What you do with the fly might turn that curiosity into all-out panic and make the muskie eat it. Reading the fish and seeing how it is reacting is often key to getting a muskie to commit and eat the fly. And experience is key to reading fish. This is where time on the water is probably the most important thing in learning these skills. Seeing muskies over and over and how they react to different situations is integral to figuring out what triggers them to eat. Here are ten things that you can do to help trigger a strike and make it easier to hook one if it eats:

1. Tip Down and Point

The biggest mistake I see while guiding muskie anglers is a blown strip-set. I estimate that 50 percent or higher of the fish that eat a fly are trout-set on. I have a saying: "If you lift the rod, you lose." A fly rod is just not stiff enough to properly set a hook. Ask any tarpon guide, and they will tell you the same thing. It might seem like there is enough power in them to get the job done, but there just isn't. Strip-set all the time, every time. It's just that simple. I have learned a lot of little tips from friends, clients, and other guides over the years. This might be one of the best: When fishing subsurface flies, keep the tip of your rod in the water about 6 inches or better. Why, you ask?

**KEEPING YOUR ROD TIP LOW
IS A KEY TO SUCCESS.**
JON LUKE

The minute a fish eats, it's simply a tap on the shoulder to remind you to keep your rod tip down and strip-set. With the tip down in the water, the minute I go to lift the rod, the water will remind me to keep that rod right there and strip-set. It's a subtle reminder that I have seen work more times than not. If an angler rips the rod tip out of the water and still tries to hook-set, they didn't deserve the fish anyway. Experience will help, just like anything else, but I have some clients that it took a long time to learn the strip-set.

The other part is to point the rod tip at your fly the best you can. A perfect example of this is when we are drift boat fishing a river. The client is usually facing the bank and casting to the structure as we quietly slide down the river. The angler casts toward a nice logjam and starts to work the fly back to the boat. As they work it back, they just keep the rod tip in the same position, not moving the rod at all. Well, the current has taken the line downriver and has put a rather nice bow in it. With a good current there is always going to be somewhat of a bow in the line no matter what you do. The job of the angler is to keep this at a minimum. By pointing the rod tip at the fly, you can greatly reduce the amount of bow in the line. You need to follow the fly downstream with the rod tip. If you don't and a fish eats, you now have 10 feet of slack line that you need to bring in before you even begin to get tight on the fish. Keep the rod tip in the water and pointed at the fly, and you will help remove a few of the obstacles that plague muskie fly anglers.

2. Keep It Moving

I use this analogy all the time, but an impala doesn't stop when a lion is chasing it. Same holds true for muskies. If a big muskie is chasing a redhorse sucker on a rock flat, the sucker is doing everything in its power to make sure it doesn't become the muskie's next meal. Your fly should do the same thing.

I like to feed a muskie a nice, easy meal. It's the old pizza analogy. Bring the pizza to the door and let them eat it. Even though you might be fishing at a slower tempo, you still can't have the fly just sitting there lifeless. I see it time and time again. A big fish will get behind the fly, and the angler will look at it in total shock and just stop fishing. This is where I come in and yell at them in a not-so-subtle way to move the damn fly. By the time this happens, though, it is usually too late and the fish has peeled off and ran back to its lair. If it's your first experience seeing a big fish follow, it can be pretty hard not to stop and look in amazement as it slowly glides behind your fly.

I once had a client that I thought was going to be a stone-cold killer muskie angler. He was an accomplished angler and had fished all over the world. He loves to fish for barracuda, so my natural instinct was that he's got this. If a muskie eats his fly, it is going to be game over. We were going along for an hour or so and nothing had moved yet. We slipped into a nice eddy with a big drop on it where I knew a few fish hung out. He placed a perfect cast into the eddy and as soon as the fly hit the seam, a giant muskie came up and smoked his fly. Game over, right? Wrong. He sat there and just stared. A big 50-inch muskie came up and did its part, but the angler didn't reciprocate. I proceeded to inform him in a not-so-subtle way that he might want to move the fly and try a strip-set. He snapped out of the trance that he was in only to find nothing left on the receiving end. He just kept staring at the eddy. Finally he said, "I can't believe there is a fish that big in here." The lesson is that even the most experienced angler can brain freeze when a big muskie eats. Keep the fly moving, and hopefully the brain freeze won't strike you.

3. Don't Burn Out

Now, I know what I said in the previous section, but there is no need to burn that fly either. One of the biggest things that I need to tell clients is to slow the fly down. A lot of anglers have the mindset that if they move the fly fast, the fish are going to have to eat it. They get in the boat and make the first cast and just start cranking on their fly line and stripping it like they were possessed. If a fly is burning through the water, there isn't really a whole lot of action in it. It's just moving straight through the water column with very little enticing action at all. It doesn't look like much of anything and it has a very slim profile under the water when you're working a fly like that. I'm not going to sit here and say it wouldn't work, because it has. I'm just saying that working a fly superfast isn't the best for a muskie. They're looking for the easy meal, and they have to really want to eat it when you're doing the speed retrieve. I believe in making it as easy as possible to eat the fly. Remember the pizza.

The other drawback to this type of retrieve is that within an hour or so your elbow will be barking like a dog. Fatigue in this type of fishing is a real issue. Now, if I see a big muskie laid up and just soaking in the sun, the speed retrieve might trigger that fish into eating. A fish that is laid up is just that, laid up. They are in either a neutral or a negative mindset. They most likely have eaten already and are just soaking up some sun while digesting their meal. If I can see the fish and it hasn't reacted to my other attempts to get it to move, the burner cast might work. Remember, this isn't going to be a long process. They'll either move at it or not. You're not blind casting for hours trying to burn it. It's a one- or two-shot proposition and then you're done. There is no worry of fatigue, and that fast retrieve might get a reaction strike. Now I go back and try to methodically deliver the pizza.

4. Tight Is Right

We have touched on it already, but this topic is that important. Simply put, you need to keep your fly line as tight as possible. We have already talked about some tricks to make that happen. There is an old saying in the Upper Midwest that goes "Slack is evil." I have even seen it posted in some of the shops out West. It always has to be in the back of your mind when you are muskie fishing. Controlling your slack is imperative to your success. As soon as you stop watching it, that is when a muskie is going to eat. They have a sixth sense about when an angler is off their game. That is when they strike. Watch your slack at all times. It will even help in all your other types of fly fishing.

5. Finish, Finish, Finish

Finish every cast, every time, no exceptions. What does that mean? It means that every cast ends with a figure eight or a turn of some kind. I can't tell you the number of muskies that I have seen get the fly pulled away from them. There is no more important cast and retrieve than the one you are currently fishing. If you're thinking about where you're going to place your next cast, you've lost it.

Here is the scenario: An angler makes a beautiful cast and works the fly wonderfully toward the boat. The angler gets the fly about 20 feet from the boat and looks up briefly to see a good pocket that they want to hit with their next cast. Instead of fishing the cast that is right in front of them, they go to pick the fly up. As soon as the fly starts to accelerate and change depths, the muskie that was following it 10 feet below charges up from the depths to eat it. It's too late. The die is cast. The next cast has started, and there is no way of stopping it. The fly is pulled out of the water with a muskie just a few feet behind it. In this case, greed is not good. If the angler would have finished the first cast with a proper figure eight, they might have induced a strike instead of a big swing and a miss. A lot of the time a muskie is lurking underneath your fly and you don't even know it. If the water is off-color or deep, there is no way of knowing that a muskie might be following your fly. If you keep cutting your cast short and not finishing each one, it will bite you sooner or later. Stay disciplined and you won't pull defeat from the jaws of victory.

6. Find the Groove

Each fly has its own groove. You can have two pretty much identical flies, but they probably both have a different groove. The groove is the speed and stripping pace you give the fly to achieve its best movement. Now, there are all kinds of different fly patterns out there. Some need to be fished faster and others slower, some with long strips and others with slow methodical strips. Whatever the fly tells you when you are fishing it is how you should fish it. A Game Changer fly is going to have to be fished a lot different than a Buford-style fly. Two Buford flies tied by the same tier are most likely going to have to be fished different even though they are the same style fly. One fly might have more deer hair than the other, one might have a slightly bigger head, another more flash, and the list goes on and on. Each fly has a sweet spot and it is up to the angler to try to find it. Knowing your fly patterns and how they are supposed to react is very helpful.

7. You're Not Beating Eggs

Your fly rod is not a whisk. I don't how many figure eight videos I've watched where the angler is spinning his fly next to the boat like he's whipping up a morning omelet. The key to a good figure eight is staying as cool and as calm as you can. That's not an

WORKING THE FLY SLOW
AND STEADY IS THE KEY.
JON LUKE

easy task when a large fish is 10 feet from your face and you're turning the fly around in a nice, big loop and changing depths as well as direction. This doesn't mean that you can't move the fly fast at the boat—it just means that you need to be in control and reading the fish. If it comes in hot and looks like it wants to eat at a little quicker tempo, that's fine. If it is slowly following the fly and not too concerned, then a slow play with enticing movements is usually the route to take. If you muskie fish for a long time, you'll see and try some very strange stuff. Staying in control is the key. If you're buzzing your fly frantically next to the boat, all sorts of things can go wrong. Handle your line properly so that when a muskie does eat, you can do something about it.

Being in the proper state of mind is also key. If you're frantically spinning the fly, hoping for the muskie to eat, your mind is most likely in a frantic state also. Calm down and work the fish. Listen to your guide if you have one. Make sure that your line is in a good position. Let the fish eat and turn. Strip-set. All of this is happening in probably a twenty-second window. If you're not calm and in the moment, it won't end well. Experience, as always, is the key. That first big muskie spinning on your figure eight is something you'll never forget. It's almost impossible to not get a little frantic. Take a deep breath and work that fish calmly. Let a cool head prevail, and put the fish in the boat.

8. Eyes on the Prize

Keep your eyes on the fly. The prize might be right behind it, and if you're not looking, you'll miss it. You would think that this tip would be pretty simple. Well, if you've been fishing for six hours and not seen a single fish, distractions are pretty easy to come by. It's hard to see the fish if you're not looking for them. I mentioned in chapter 4 that good sunglasses are key, and they help more than you know. Distraction and boredom are the biggest enemies of the muskie angler. Pretty soon you'll find yourself looking at the birds, looking for that next cast, chatting with your buddies, fiddling with your line, or just being in zombie mode. It's going to happen. It is part of the game. The biggest thing is to try to stay as focused as you can. You have to be looking at your fly at all times. If you're turning into a zombie, take a break. There is no shame in that. I would rather have a client sit down for a good break to get their head right than to fish like they're just going through the motions. I see this a lot. If you need a break, take one.

When I get the boat into a spot that I know is really good, I'll let the anglers know. I tell them that I need their A game in here. That lets them know that they have to fish it with the upmost attention to detail. This also holds true for bite windows. You want to be focused and in the game during these windows. The more experience you have on your body of water, the better you'll get at knowing when to turn it up a notch. Now, you should be at an 11 all the time, but we all know that just isn't possible. Keep your eye on the prize, which is your fly. You never know when Mr. Big is going to show up.

9. Strip It Real Good

For the beginner, this might be as good advice as you can get. I was talking to one of my guides, Russ, about the book and asked him what was the one piece of advice he'd give the beginner about working the fly. He told me this, and I thought it was really good: When you're working the fly, strip like you mean it. When you strip the fly, put some power behind it. A lot of the time, a fish will eat the fly and you won't see it. If you strip the fly with purpose and the muskie eats it, you might have a chance to put the fly into its jaw. You'd be surprised how many logs anglers hang up on that turn out to be muskies. Often a client will say, "I'm hung up." They're afraid to lose the fly, so they don't set the hook. I'll begin to move the boat to retrieve the fly, and that is when the log starts to move and with it an opportunity lost. When working your fly, work it with purpose, and if it stops for any reason, set the damn hook. I'd rather lose a few flies throughout the season than perhaps the fish of a lifetime.

10. Practice

All of the previous tips are nothing without practice and time on the water. They all need to become second nature for the angler. Muscle memory is a wonderful thing. Remember that practice doesn't make perfect, but perfect practice makes perfect. Fish with purpose the right way, and the learning curve will shrink and that muscle memory will form good habits, not bad ones. If you buy or tie a new fly, test it. Take it out and work it to see how it swims. Don't waste your time when you're fishing trying to figure out how the fly is supposed to look. I spend a lot of time at the boat ramp in the winter testing and working flies. When I hit the water during the season, I know how each fly works and what it takes to make it move the way I want it to.

You'll learn so much with practice that it is well worth the time spent. When you go to your practice session, go with a game plan. Make a mental list of the things that you'd like to work on. Just do a couple of things. Don't make it some big marathon session—fifteen to twenty minutes a few times a week will go a long way toward putting that trophy in the boat.

FLY THEORY AND ACTION

This is kind of like opening Pandora's box. There are a lot of theories out there about what makes a good fly and what action is the best. Let me just say this: There is no right or wrong answer to any of these questions. Once again it comes down to confidence. What has worked for you and what the fish are telling you are the two most important things to consider. Remember, the fish are always telling us something. Most of the time it isn't what we want to hear, but they're definitely communicating with their pursuer. I look to my friends that fish for muskies with conventional gear for most of my insights. There's a lot more of them than there are fly anglers. They cover a hell of a lot more water too. Many of my theories have come from talking to them and seeing what is the latest and greatest. Some of the most successful fly guides out there are old conventional-gear guides. They know what works on that side of it and try to implement what works on the fly side.

One of the most successful muskie baits in the last fifteen years is the double-bladed bucktail inline spinner known as the Double Cowgirl. It hit the water in 2003 and has been responsible for a ton of fish over the 50-inch mark. What makes the Cowgirl so different? Just that it was completely different from any other lure out there at the time. It has what I consider the most important factor in any type of muskie bait: the underwater disturbance that it creates. If you haven't had a chance to throw one, I suggest you do so. The minute that you start reeling it in, the light will immediately go on. The entire rod shakes with the vibration that the double blades cause. The other added feature is that the inventors replaced the bucktail with a pack of Flashabou, creating a thumping spinner with a ton of flash. It was a deadly combination and continues to be.

The dilemma with the fly rod is that you can never duplicate the speed of conventional gear. To get the blades on a Cowgirl to thump, you have to have enough speed on them to get them turning. We will never be able to produce the amount of speed needed to make blades turn, let alone be able to cast them. As a fly designer and angler, I'm always asking what can be done with a fly to get that thumping vibration under the water column like an inline spinner. All that the blades of an inline spinner are doing is misplacing water and causing a vibration to go out from it. In my fly design, that is the first thing that I want to do. I want a fly to displace as much water as possible. I want it to thump and cause some kind of disturbance. That disturbance will be picked up by the lateral line in a muskie and hopefully get it interested in my offering. This is why I'm such a big proponent of large flies here in the Upper Midwest. I want to ring the dinner bell as loudly as I possibly can. If that muskie is

Gabe inspecting the goods

JON LUKE

at all close to my fly, it will feel the presence of it before it even sees it. I want the muskie to feel it and then come looking for it. I've just triggered its hunting instinct and hopefully it comes hunting for my fly.

Another important thing with muskie flies is that the fly should still move even when it isn't. How can that happen? Any good muskie fly has movement, even after you're done stripping it. If it doesn't kick or roll after you have stripped it, simply put, I'm not going to fish it. Movement after motion in the fly is paramount. The kick after the strip is what I feel is the most important factor when it comes to a fly. If the fly doesn't kick, it's just a bunch of hair and feathers getting pulled through the water.

During the first Orvis Muskie School, Pete Kutzer brought a bunch of flies for the students to try. They were nice flies, but they didn't have the kick that I like in my flies. We casted them and I could tell that they did nothing in the water except go straight. The second you stopped your strip, they just sat there and sank. Remember what I said about keeping your fly moving. Even when a baitfish is dying, it still has movement. It might be the subtlest of movement, but at least it still has some life in it. I want my fly to be working every second of a cast, even if I'm not. How this is achieved is by getting a kick from the fly at the end of the strip. The death roll is what I call it. It looks like a baitfish that is barely keeping itself alive. The struggle of the fly makes it an easy mark for a willing muskie. The other thing that is always moving on a good fly is the Flashabou and other synthetic materials. New materials are being developed and discovered every year and are really bringing life to large muskie flies. There has to be motion after the movement of the fly.

Since we can't imitate an inline spinner really well with a fly, I asked my conventional-gear buddies what was the best action that I could achieve with a fly. They all agreed that it would be to imitate a glide or jerk bait. If you're not familiar with a glide bait, it's a bait that runs underwater and you jerk to give it a walk-the-dog action. All of the conventional-tackle guides that I have talked to think this is the number one action there is. A simple walk-the-dog or zigzag. It seems like muskies really key in on this action, which is similar to the movement a wounded or suffering baitfish makes.

This action is very easy to duplicate with a fly. It is the one that I fish most often throughout the season. Also, it is easy to control. You can have a very big walk-the-dog action or a subtle one. Some flies can really produce the big kick that you might be looking for, while in other flies the kick can be minimal. Finding that perfect kick for the situation is, as always, an experience issue. The more time on the water you have, the better feel you'll get for what a particular situation calls for. This is another lesson that I learned from my conventional counterparts. Sometimes they want to run bigger blades on their bucktails, and at other times they are scaling them down and running a smaller version. A lot of this depends on weather, wind, etc. After a cold front, most guys will slow everything down a bit and go somewhat smaller, since the fish tend to be a little more lethargic and less aggressive. Picking the right fly for the situation is no different than a conventional angler picking the right style of bait. They just have a bigger sample to pick from. We are very limited in the styles of flies we can throw.

After all that talk, I'll admit that I know several serious muskie anglers that will run the same fly the entire fall season. It's a big walk-the-dog-type fly with a redhorse sucker coloration. Their theory is that red-

Which one will produce the beast?
JON LUKE

horses are the muskie's main diet during the fall, so why fish anything different? You know what? It works. It's just like anything in muskie fishing: Don't get wrapped around the axle. If you overthink anything in this game, you can get paralysis by analysis. Muskies will sooner or later prove your theories wrong. I have said that there is no way that any self-respecting muskie would eat a fly like that and had to eat my words. The action of the fly and fishing it diligently are the key factors that I would emphasize more than color or size.

Topwater Action

Fishing topwater flies is very different from fishing subsurface flies. Fishing topwater usually occurs during the warmer months of the year, when the muskies' metabolism is very fast due to the warmer water temperatures. They are a little more active and seem more willing to hit topwater presentations. I like to work a big popper or boiler very aggressively. I just keep popping it loud and quick to draw attention to the fly, and hopefully the aggressive nature of the fly will trigger a strike. There isn't a whole lot that you can do differently when working a big popper or boiler. You can change speeds, the length of pops, and the size of the popper, but that's about it. Let the fish tell you what you need.

As for diver-type flies, I fish them a little slower just because you have to. They need to come back up to the surface so that you can pop them again. I do, however, give them a pretty good rip to make a bunch of noise and a nice bubble line. A diver is slower, but you can also experiment with the size of the fly and the speed and intervals between the dives.

Topwater fishing can be a hoot. It is the ultimate when it comes to seeing the fish and watching their reaction. If it's a dog day of summer and you're looking to have some fun, I would definitely give it a try. Pop and hold on. Things can get pretty exciting. One thing to remember is to let them eat the fly.

Fly selection and action is a very personal thing. Like I've said numerous times, it's all about confidence. You need to be confident in what you're fishing, and that positive energy will transfer into better fishing. Keep experimenting with all your flies and the different ways that you fish them. You'll settle into a nice groove and be well rewarded for your hard work and experimentation.

Kip Notes

- Practice your cast and your execution in working the fly. You have the proper equipment—now it's about time on the water and perfecting your on-the-water skills. The effort that you put into your practice will pay off. Serious muskie anglers aren't part-timers.
- Find a fly or a pattern that you have confidence in and fish it. It's all about the confidence factor. If you believe that a certain fly is going to catch fish, you're already ahead of the curve.
- Keep that line as tight as possible. When go-time comes, I want as tight of a connection to that fly as I can get. If you're playing catch-up with your fly line, your chances of hooking a muskie diminish greatly.
- Keep the fly moving.
- Finish every cast as if your life depends on it.
- Practice, practice, practice!

CHAPTER SIX

CLOSING THE DEAL

Before I started guiding full-time, I spent a lot of time in sales. Every manager that I ever worked for would ask, "What is your close rate? How come you're not closing the deal? What can we do to close this deal?" It was always about closing the deal. The other thing that was always stressed in our sales meetings was, "Are you building a quality relationship with your customers?" So what the heck does any of this have to do with muskie fishing? It has everything to do with muskie. How good your closing rate is has a direct relationship to how well you know your customers. My managers would always ask, "How well do you know your customers?" You should know their birthday, wife's name, kids' names, what school their kids attend, what hobbies they like, what music they listen to, and most importantly to me, if they hunt and fish. The managers' theory was the more you know about your clients, the harder it will be for them to buy from someone else. Let's flip it around to fishing, and I think that it will make perfect sense.

There is a fish that I have chased for about ten years now. I call her Big Betty, and I have only had her hooked solidly once. It was by a veteran who was on the veterans' trip that I try to organize every fall. This guy had never picked up a fly rod before. He learned it very quickly, though, and was soon dialed in. We got to the spot that Betty calls home, and I didn't say anything. I just told him where to cast. He fired a couple casts in the seam, but nothing. On the next cast he was stripping it in and just quietly looked back at me and calmly said, "Hey, I think I have one."

Now, I hadn't seen Betty all year, and she is a very slippery fish. He stuck her really good. I stood up as his rod bucked with the giant on it. I shouted instructions on fighting her. Then it happened. I saw her with the fly in her mouth and just started shaking. I knew her as well as you can when it comes to a big fish like this. You might only see them a few times a year—they are just that different and smart. I could hardly contain myself knowing that it was her. She had followed my presentations many times. She had blown up on a topwater presentation, and shown herself just enough

Bowing to the freshwater king: A tiger muskie makes his presence felt.

BEN LUKE

to keep haunting me. We did battle for what seemed like ten hours, but probably was only a few minutes. She looked like she was beat, and I told the client to give her a little pressure to turn her head toward the boat and she would most likely just slide into the net. He did what he was told to perfection. He gave her a little gentle pull, and that is when I almost threw up. Betty had one last gasp in her. She jumped out of the water, shook her head, and spit the fly like it was nothing. I have never been as heartbroken on a fish as I was that exact moment. I slammed the net down and started ranting, and then sat down with my head in my hands almost weeping.

That moment still haunts me. I know that I'm dating myself, but I felt like the ski jumper in the opening of ABC's *Wide World of Sports*. For all you younger folks, just google it and you'll get it. The vet turned and told me that it was the coolest thing that he had ever experienced and was all smiles. It made me feel a little bit better but not much. *I didn't close the deal*. That was the biggest deal that I've ever had in my entire life and it slipped through my hands. It was all on me. The vet did everything that I told him to do and he performed flawlessly. I'm the guy that told him to turn her head and we could net her. I guess I didn't know my customer as well as I should have. If I'd just given her a little more time, we would have had her. I wanted the deal so bad that I rushed to close it, and it cost me and my client the fish of a lifetime.

In my defense, a fish that big is really hard to get to know. They get that big for a reason. They're smart, they don't eat very often, and they're extremely shy. They almost become a subspecies of muskie. If you talk to any longtime muskie guide, they will tell you the same thing. When a fish gets over 50 inches, they turn into a different sort of animal. Just think of all the things that they have seen and stored in their brains. I'm not saying that they have memories like you and I have, but they do get conditioned. How many lures, flies, and boats have they seen in their lives? I've heard some guides say that those big fish know when a motor approaches their area, and it's never a good thing. They just can't be raised. That sounds like an old guide wives' tale, but who knows? That fish didn't get 50-plus inches by accident.

So, what can an angler do to learn about his customer, the muskie? Spend as much time as possible on the water and learn. Guides that work the same lakes over and over for years can tell you countless stories of fish they have chased over their careers. For example, one of my guide friends knew that a certain set of rocks every September just before a full moon always held a certain fish. He would see that fish every year during that event, and almost every year he managed to catch it. The last time he landed it, the fish was 54½ inches. That's knowing your customer.

As you can see, closing the deal has more to do with experience than anything else. Learning how to read fish, what to do when they eat, how to trigger them to eat—it's all about setting up the close. I've had plenty of fish, as I call it, commit suicide. That is, they do everything perfect and the angler basically just has to hold their rod and fight the fish. They come up from the side of the fly, eat it with a vengeance, and keep going away from the boat. All the angler has to do is pin the line against the rod cork and let the fish do the rest. They swim away, the line gets tight, and they basically hook themselves. Life is grand when that happens, but those closes are few and far between. That close is like a Girl Scout selling cookies to her grandmother. It's a sure thing. The real skill comes in when the angler has to have nerves of steel, read the fish, think fast, and make that muskie eat their presentation. That is what closing is all about. Seeing how various fish react to different situations is how you learn the art of the close. I'll say this, though, even after years of fishing, you'll always have one that will do something so weird that you just sit there and shake your head. They are muskies after all.

THE EAT

This is why you fish muskies. It's all about the eat. Seeing the top of the food chain come up and destroy your fly is one of the greatest thrills in all of fly fishing. I've had large muskies come up from the bottom of the river and open their mouths. It looks as if a white five-gallon bucket has just engulfed your fly. It is surreal to watch it happen. I've also had clients that thought they were stuck on a log, only to have it turn out to be a large muskie. An eat can happen any way that you can imagine. It can also happen any way you can't imagine.

There's not a lot I can tell you to prepare you for when a big muskie eats. I've been guiding for them for many years and I still get jacked up when I see a big fish eat. When the entire boat gasps all at the same time, you know it's a good one. It is

When the goal is achieved, the feeling is pretty special.
KIP VIETH

always going to give you pause, and sometimes that's not a bad thing. I'm not going to say every eat is different, but few are the same. If it was up to me, they'd all be the same. That would make all our jobs a heck of a lot easier. This is one part of knowing your customer that is almost impossible to know. They can eat your fly coming at you, going away from you, from underneath, over the top, sideways, you name it—sooner or later it will happen to you. Knowing what to do next is the real test.

Sometimes it doesn't happen. You just look at the fish as it swims away, salute it, and say it won. It stinks, there is no doubt about it, but it happens. I always tell my clients that they are most likely going to miss their first muskie. It's what you do the second, third, and fiftieth time that matters. You always have to be learning. Growing nerves of steel helps too, but good luck with that. If you do remain that calm, I say quit the game. It's no fun if you remain too calm.

Let's talk about what goes down when that fateful moment arrives, and how you can close the deal. The first thing to remember is that if you can get a solid hook-set on the fish, the chances of landing it are pretty good. That is the first hurdle and probably the most important in the close. Without a quality hook-set, you stand little or no chance of actually landing the fish. We've talked about it a lot, but it is the critical thing to closing. One of the biggest mistakes that beginner muskie fly anglers make is trout-setting. Lifting the rod is the curse of death. If you lift your rod to set the hook, you are not going to close the deal 95 percent of the time. Strip-setting is the only way you're going to get your fly properly set in a muskie's hard mouth.

One tip that a fishing buddy gave me was to keep the rod tip in the water at least a foot or so. The resistance the water puts on your rod as you set the hook is a gentle reminder to strip-set and not lift the rod. When you go to lift the rod, the water will remind you to strip-set. It's a pretty simple trick, but it seems to work more often than not, especially for a new muskie angler.

You can do everything perfectly, but if you don't drive that hook into their mouth, none of it will matter. Think about that for a minute. You can present your fly perfectly, have a tight line, have the rod pointed at the fish, no trout-set, but if you don't strip-set like your fishing life depended on it, it's all for nothing. You may as well stop reading this book. It comes down to that three-second period when you have to strike. If you blow that opportunity, the chances of you holding that fish for your Instagram post are slim to none. It's that important.

Don't get me wrong—you're going to blow it, a lot. Everyone does, but that doesn't mean you just overlook this aspect of the game. It is the difference between being average or good. In muskie fishing, there is never great. I've seen who I think is the best muskie angler blow a few. It happens. Remember, great is the enemy of good and no one is that special. Muskies have a way of humbling you, as I've said before. They win more than I care to admit. You have to block that out of your mind, however, and go about your business as if that isn't even a factor. The most important thing is to never panic, which is a tall order when something that big eats your fly.

Getting a muskie to eat your fly is the goal, but it's what you do with that eat that will tell the true tale. As I have said over and over, it's all about keeping a direct connection to the fish. When an eat and hook-set go wrong, it is the connection that's to blame about 90 percent of the time. What I mean by this is that there is usually too much slack in the system to get a quality hook-set on the fish. This has everything to do with how the fish eats the fly. Like we talked about earlier, if the fish eats and moves away from the angler, it's pretty much a done deal. The tricky part is when the fish doesn't follow directions and eats the fly coming at you sideways, on the figure eight, or in any number of different scenarios. You just never know how or when they will eat in the process. Being ready for it at all times is key. No one can really know when that eat will come. It can be after the first strip or at the tip of the fly rod on a figure eight. It can happen almost anywhere in between too. I guess if I had to pick a perfect moment, it would be that third or fourth strip. The line will most likely be tight and the fish is far enough from the boat that you can somewhat manage it, if that is possible. Once again, that is the perfect scenario and it seldom happens like that.

The trickiest eats to turn into landed fish are those where it is difficult to get the line tight, particularly when a muskie comes up from behind the fly. Often they eat the fly and then just glide for a bit right at you. You strip like a crazy person and don't get enough of a strip-strike on it, but get just enough of a strike to tell the fish that something isn't right. It'll turn away from you and spit the fly, and all you're left with is a faint glimpse of the fish as it swims away. It's in my opinion the hardest eat to convert into a boated fish. You just never seem to get tight enough to really drive that hook into their iron jaw. Here's where patience and nerves of steel come into play. If you can get this down, you will have graduated with a PhD in muskie fishing. This maneuver is the most difficult to pull off when it comes to an eat: It is simply waiting. It takes nerves of steel, as I have said. When a muskie eats your fly, it isn't going to let it go for a while unless something tells it this isn't right. It wants to crush its prey and eat it.

I was chasing redfish a few years back, and my guide provided a very valuable lesson. On that trip, I had a 28-pound redfish eat my fly. Now, this happened right after muskie season had just wrapped up here in the Upper Midwest, so my strip-set game was in top form. When the red ate my fly, I set with one of the best strip-sets of my life. The fish showed very little reaction to the fly getting driven into its mouth. Redfish have a much softer mouth than muskies do, so I was pretty sure that I had stuck him. I just kept strip-setting because of my muskie experience, thinking that I wasn't tight enough and that the fly wasn't in its mouth. It was really hooked after

When they want to eat it, they're going to eat it. The rest is up to you.
KIP VIETH

the first strip-set but didn't start its run until it was by the boat. Once it realized that something wasn't right, it headed for open water. We landed the fish, and it was incredible—one of the highlights of my fishing career. I sat there for a minute, and remember this is right after muskie season, and asked my guide why the fish didn't take off after I stuck him the first time. He looked at me and asked, "What do redfish eat every day?" I replied, "Crabs and shrimp for the most part, correct?" He said, "Exactly," and went on to explain that those are things that poke and stab the fish when they are getting eaten. A little hook isn't much more than what they experience every day. That made perfect sense to me. A hook isn't much more than a crab pinching them as they try to eat it.

Now fast-forward to this fall. A client had a muskie eat just as I described earlier. The muskie came up from behind on the fly, ate it, and glided straight at the angler. The client stripped like a madman and never really got as tight as he needed to be. It happens. Like I said, that eat is difficult at best. About the only way to get tight on this type of eat is to wait, for what can seem like an hour, for the fish to turn and swim away. When the adrenaline is at 11, this is almost impossible. I explained this to the client. On those eats it's best to just let the fish turn a little to get a solid hook-set on it. The client asked, "Won't the muskie spit the fly out once it feels the hook or something else in the fly?" My answer was, "What do muskies eat?" Suckers, bluegills, ducks, muskrats, ciscoes—all have bones and hard things in them. They aren't going to spit it out right away. They want to crush it, kill it, and then eat it. You have time to let that fish turn and give you a better opportunity to get your line tight and drive the hook home. I'm not saying this will ever be easy, but it is the best way to try to close on a fish that eats coming at you. Seldom will they continue to swim toward the boat. They kick it in, eat the fly, glide a bit, and then hopefully turn away or to the side. This is where you need to lay the timber to them. Strip-set good, hold on, and let the fun begin.

I have just six words of advice to wrap up the eat section: strip-set, strip-set, and then strip-set again!

THE FOLLOW

I think Charles Dickens sums up a muskie follow in the opening line of his classic novel *A Tale of Two Cities* better than anyone: "It was the best of times, it was the worst of times, it was the age of wisdom, it was the age of foolishness, it was the epoch of belief, it was the epoch of incredulity, it was the season of Light, it was the season of Darkness, it was the spring of hope, it was the winter of despair, we had everything before us, we had nothing before us, we were all going direct to Heaven, we were all going direct the other way . . ."

If you can figure it out from the quote, follows are nice, but eats are better. Follows are a double-edged sword. It's great to see a fish, but man can it be frustrating. Now, if we've been at it for a day and a half and haven't seen a thing, I'll take the follow. At least I know that there are fish around and that they are somewhat interested. The fish is looking, and that's a start. On the other hand, if we've been fishing for that day and a half and have seen fourteen fish with nothing to show for it, that is when I start to lose it a bit. I don't know what is worse—not seeing anything or having fish flip you the fin over and over. Both are bad, but I guess I'd rather see fish than not. Sooner or later one of those fish is going to eat. As my buddy Troy used to say when I first started muskie fishing, never leave fish to find fish.

Trying to turn that follow into an eat can be a daunting task at times. Follow experience is only achieved by doing. Time on the water, my friends. The more muskies that you see, the better you will be able to read them. It is a skill that only comes with time. I've seen some really weird stuff over the years. I have even poked a muskie with the rod tip because it was acting so bizarre. You'll see some pretty cool stuff when muskies follow, and that time on the water is key to learning how to manipulate them into eating. Personally, as I've said before, just give me a big eat about 30 feet from the boat and I'm good.

Fall is when I do a lot of my muskie guiding. Smallmouth fishing has slowed and I switch my focus to muskies, and for good reason. The approaching winter get the fish more aggressive. I don't experience as many follows as, say, a summer angler. In the fall my experience has been that muskies seem to eat more than follow. Here comes the word *usually*. That's usually true, but there are always exceptions. Some years it seems like every muskie follows and then eats at the boat. Other years you might only have a handful of follows with most of the eats coming farther away from the boat. Just know that usually it depends on the year. What's usual this year might not be usual the next.

Let's be very clear: Follows are an extremely important part of the game. They can set you up for a great deal of success if executed properly. But there is also the flip side: If you're not on your A game during a follow, things can go wrong in a hurry. Being aware of your surroundings and knowing what to look for are as important as anything while you're muskie fishing. What you do if a fish is following your fly sets up everything. If I can see that fish following my fly, I can now begin to work the fly to try to close the deal. It is all about getting that fish to trigger mode and getting it to eat your fly. What you do as the fish follows the fly is crucial in getting it to eat.

One of my guide buddies gave some sound advice to a client a few years back. He said that when you're driving your car, you don't look at the steering wheel, do you? Now, you might look down at your speedometer or other gauges as you drive, but if you just stared at the instrument panel, you'd end up crashing into something. The outcome would not be desirable. You need to be looking down the road and off to the sides. You're trying to anticipate the next turn and looking for any danger that might be out there. Muskie fishing is the same way. Yes, you need to look at your fly to make sure that it is running OK, but don't just stare at it. The majority of the time, the angler should be looking out for danger. In other words, you should be scanning for that follow. If your mind is concentrated on your driving/fishing, there is less that can go wrong. If you are more aware of your surroundings and less focused on your fly, you stand a better chance of seeing a muskie come after your

Everyone is happy, even the guide, when a plan comes together.
KIP VIETH

fly. It won't be a surprise. You will be able to put your plan into action and avoid undesirable outcomes.

What should you be looking for when you are scanning for a muskie? Basically, anything different. It's just that simple. If something doesn't look right or is out of place, you should immediately follow protocol. Often it's a shadow behind the fly, a change in water color around the fly, a flash of white, or a slight push of water that is different. Most of the time it's just a hunch or gut feeling. The more you fish, the more of these you'll have. You just know something isn't as it should be.

The faster you can see a muskie following your fly, the better. It's always nice to have as much time as possible to try to trigger the muskie to eat the fly. The best thing you can do to help with this is to wear a good pair of polarized sunglasses. I will argue for using good polarized sunglasses as long as I continue to guide. A good, and I mean good, quality pair of polarized sunglasses might be one of the most beneficial pieces of equipment that any angler can have. I know that they can be expensive and everyone has to live within a budget, but you owe it to yourself and your fishing to get the best pair that you can afford. Most of the leading brands have excellent warranties and will help you find the best glasses for you. I always say if it comes down to buying a few extra flies or glasses, get the glasses. They will help you catch more fish than a few more flies, a new fly box, an extra spool, or any number of things you might spend your money on. They are that important, and if you don't think so now, sooner or later you will. If you see ten more fish a year, think of what that will do to your chances of catching that fish of a lifetime. Make the investment and if you can, get a few different-colored lenses for different fishing situations.

If a muskie looks aggressive, it is. An aggressive muskie has that killer look in its eyes. Its body is positioned differently and it swims with more purpose. A muskie that gives your fly an aggressive look usually means business. It's when you see that look that a follow often goes wrong. A lot of times the muskie will catch you off-guard. If you're surprised, you'll have a tendency stop the fly, and if you stop the fly, you've lost for the most part. When you get that look from a muskie, you must never pause. Nothing will turn a muskie off faster. I've used the analogy before, but an impala never slows or stops when a lion is chasing it. A muskie's prey doesn't stop or slow either. I can't tell you the number of times that an angler has seen a big fish follow and just froze. Nothing will shut a muskie down faster than that. If it's your first big follow, it probably is going to happen. The more you practice this in your mind and on the water, the more prepared you'll be.

So, what is the follow protocol that I spoke of earlier? It's just a game of keep-away. I'm trying to keep that fly away from the muskie that is stalking it. I'm also trying to trigger that eat away from the boat if at all possible. If I can, I try to avoid a boatside eat. A lot can go wrong at the boat, so the farther out the muskie eats my fly, the better my odds are of getting it to the net. That being said, I'll take an eat anywhere I can get it. Know that the fly has to keep moving, if not sped up a bit. A follow sets up your alternative move. It can be speeding the fly up, moving it in a different manner, a figure eight, or just a big turn. It depends on reading the fish. The minute you see a muskie behind your fly, you have to immediately start thinking, What can I do to get this muskie to trigger and eat my fly? What is it going to take, and how am I going to manipulate my fly to make that muskie eat it?

A lot has to do with reading the fish and seeing just how aggressive it is. If the muskie hasn't eaten your fly yet, you know that you have to do something different. You need to change that muskie's mood from neutral to attack mode. The muskie has already expended some energy moving to the fly and is following it. We know that it is somewhat interested. Now the dance begins and the game of keep-away starts. As soon as I see a muskie behind the fly, I am thinking about two things: speed and erratic movements. I begin to increase the speed of the fly. I don't go crazy—I just start moving it with more purpose. I like to gauge the muskie's interest with that first move. If the fish begins to speed up with the fly, I know that it is getting hotter. I will often then begin a directional change of some kind. I will make an erratic move. I will move the fly to the side or to a different depth. This change in direction is often the thing that flips the trigger. I have sped up the fly and changed its path. The fly now looks like something that doesn't like what is behind it. It is looking for the nearest exit to escape the pending doom. If the muskie is serious about eating, this is often when it'll trigger and eat the fly. If not and the fly gets to the boat, I

PAYING ATTENTION TO WHAT
IS GOING ON UNDER THE
WATER IS AS IMPORTANT AS
NOTICING WHAT IS TAKING
PLACE ABOVE.
JON LUKE

then start a big turn, into a figure eight. If the follow goes wrong on a hot fish, it's not going to eat.

The other thing to keep in mind is that you don't have to see the fish to make that fly move in an erratic way. When retrieving your fly, give it some kind of different movement. You can give it a burst of speed, a directional change, or a change in depth. This is the reason I like the walk-the-dog type of flies. They move through the water very erratically, and you don't have to manipulate them a great deal to get them to bob and weave. That motion can be deadly. Remember, we're just trying to figure out what is going to trigger a muskie to eat. Every cast should have some kind of erratic movement in it. Throw them a slider when they're expecting a fastball.

All follows are good in one way or another. Every time you see a muskie, it's a good thing. If it slow-rolls in or just lurks behind the fly, all is not lost. You now have an address for that fish. The more addresses of muskies you put in your book, the better. If I get an address in the fall, the chances are pretty good that a fish will be at that address most, if not all, of the season. The same holds true at other times of the year. If I move a muskie in the middle of the summer, I know that fish is going to be nearby until the water cools. A spot that had fish in it one year usually will have fish in it the following year, be it spring, summer, or fall. Muskies are a fish of patterns. Those spots hold fish for a reason. Unless something drastic changes, that particular spot is going to be a good place to start. Having a mental book of muskie addresses is gold. If I know where a muskie is calling home, I can ring the dinner bell every time I'm out fishing.

THE FINISH

As we have discussed, all casts need to be finished. You finish each cast with a big turn at the boat. I don't harp on a figure eight after every cast, but you need to at least make a big turn. I have seen muskies jump out of the water to eat a fly that was being picked up instead of turned. When an angler decides to pick up the fly before they turn it at the boat, they are doing the two things that trigger a fish: increasing speed and giving the fly an erratic move. The muskie is following below and away from the fly. The angler decides to not work the fly to the boat and begins their cast. This causes the fly to speed up and change directions. For a muskie that is thinking about eating, a speed increase and depth change is all it takes to trigger the eat. The only problem with that is that a fly in the air is hard for a muskie to eat. All that is left is a big swirl and a muskie wondering where the heck its meal just went. The muskie was ready to eat, but the angler didn't let it. Always turn that fly at the end of every cast.

You have to close. Often the figure eight or a simple turn is what is needed to close out a muskie. It doesn't have to be a figure eight either. I have learned from other guides that they use a simple oval or circle. It makes perfect sense. Often when doing a figure eight, the fly will stall if you're not proficient at it. A simple oval is easier to do and gives the fly a nice, steady action when a fish is that close. Let's just say you can get a little rattled, and why make things any harder than they already are?

The Figure Eight

During the summer months, a high percentage of muskies that are landed are hooked during an erratic move at the boat. Knowing how to figure eight is a skill that you need to have if you want to be a good muskie angler. It isn't that complicated—it just takes practice. Remember earlier in the book? That's right, it's all about practice, and the figure eight is a very simple thing to practice. The sale is right on the table, and it is up to you to convert it. If your sales pitch, your figure eight, isn't ready for prime time, a simple oval will do. It's better to give some kind of sales pitch as opposed to none at all. As is often said, perfect is the enemy of good. If you have practiced the maneuver, you'll be more comfortable with it, and when it's go-time, it will be second nature. Does it happen every time? Heck no. It is, however, the most exciting of all eats, and you have more control over the process than at any other time in a cast. The fly is at the rod tip, and it is up to you to move and manipulate it so that the muskie will eat it. If you have practiced your figure eights, things will go smoothly, and the deal just might get closed.

I'd like to talk a little about the reality of a day muskie fishing. When I'm guiding clients, I don't ask them to figure eight every cast. It's just not a realistic expectation. I don't know in the grand scheme of things if it is always the right thing to do. Most clients after several hours of fishing just simply start to fade. I have talked a lot about discipline, and this is where it starts to show itself. Anglers start missing figure eights and start picking up their casts early. When the fly comes to the boat, it at least has to be turned in an L or J turn. *It must be done every cast!* Muskies follow your fly more than you think. They might be 10 feet underneath it and you never see them. If you don't put some type of erratic movement into your fly at the end of each cast, you're going to cost yourself a fish. This is the one thing that I probably correct my clients on the most when I'm out guiding. I have the 3 o'clock rule. If you haven't gotten it by 3 o'clock in the afternoon, then you're not going to. You're probably sick of me correcting you by then anyway. The first fish that you miss because you didn't turn your fly will do more teaching than I ever could. Just turn every cast and everything will be fine. It takes discipline, but in the end it will pay off.

Almost all of my trips are on rivers. If an angler does a complicated figure eight after every cast, they might miss a spot that had a muskie sitting on it. It's all about covering the water, and if you're spinning an eight after every cast, you might miss the fish of a lifetime. There is a balance that you have to reach. Every cast needs to be finished at least with a turn—it just doesn't have to be a drawn-out figure eight every time. Some guides will probably argue this point, and they are probably right more than they are wrong. I'm just a realist. Getting someone to figure eight every cast is a tall order. If I was new to muskie fishing, I would make it a point to try to figure eight each cast. It's a great time to get that all-important experience.

I play a game on each trip. When I get to one of my productive spots where I know there are fish, I simply say, "I need your A game here." Every cast needs to be finished with a figure eight. You need to be as focused as you can be when I say "A game." This is not to say that you shouldn't be alert all the time, but I know how hard

GABE COACHING THE BOYS ON
THE PROPER FIGURE EIGHT
AARON OTTO

that is to do. You'll know after fishing for a while where your A game spots are and where you need to bring your game up another level. The more you fish a river or lake, the more A game spots you'll develop. You'll also find that spots that you thought were A game locations actually are not. Every year I have a spot that I swear holds a big fish in it. I work that spot hard and intensely and it never comes to fruition. I'm a hunch player. If it looks good it probably is, but not all hunches play out. Now, there could be a large fish in that hole, but it never showed itself. Your confidence fades and that A game spot now moves to a B+. Keep fishing it, but don't spend too much time in it until you see a fish deserving of an A.

The figure eight is not that complicated. It needs to be practiced a lot so that it becomes second nature. When a big fish is bearing down on your fly, it's very easy to come unglued. The more hours that are spent practicing the maneuver, the better. You can become pretty good in a short amount of time, but it takes years to really make it second nature.

A few tricks will go a long way in closing the deal that is right in front of you. The first is to have a good body and rod position. When the fly comes in to the boat, you want to be facing directly at it with your rod tip pointed right at the fly. No slack should be in the line, and the leader should be right into the rod tip. Reach out with the rod to start your first maneuver as far out from the boat as you can. This is why I like longer rods. I also stick the rod tip into the water—it gives me more control over the fly and the depth in which it is running. I like to try to start my turn of the fly as far from the boat as I can, while still maintaining control. I want the muskie concentrating on the fly and not the boat in front of it. Often if the fish is aggressive that first turn is the one that is going to get it to eat the fly. As we have discussed, it is frequently that first erratic move that will trigger the muskie into eating or showing itself. If that first initial L turn doesn't trigger the eat, go right into a figure eight.

There are many opinions on how to do a figure eight. I will tell you what I think works best in my fishing situations. There are no rules when it comes to a figure eight. It seems like every fish is a bit different, and what worked one time won't work the next. There are just a lot of basics, and from those you can fine-tune your figure eight to what works best for you.

The first thing to remember is not to slow down. In the turn the fly has a tendency to slow a bit—that is simple physics. If anything, speed it up a bit. Remember, we're trying to play keep-away. The biggest mistake you can make is a stall of some kind. You want to keep the fly moving at all times. As long as the fish is following your fly, you need to keep it moving. I have seen muskies follow a fly at least six times and then decide to eat. Even if the fish disappears, I always turn it a few more times. Sometimes they like to sulk under the boat out of sight. Work the figure eight a few more times, and maybe try something different. Speed it up, slow it down, change depths—just do something that is different. This will often get the fish to show back up and eat your presentation. If it stops following your fly, you really have nothing to lose. Shake it up a bit and see if you can bring the fish back.

The next thing to remember while doing the figure eight is to make wide turns. It's the old aircraft carrier analogy: Something that big just can't turn on a dime. It

A tiger muskie that fell for a well-executed figure eight

JON LUKE

takes a little room for it to maneuver. By making wide steady turns, you're giving that big fish a chance to stay on track and eat the fly. If you work the fly like you're whisking up an omelet, it is hard for them to track and turn on the fly. I have seen clients and YouTube videos of anglers spinning a fly like they're having some kind of panic attack. I'm not going to say you'll never get an eat by doing that—after all, they're muskies—but if you're spinning a fly like that, you're just not in as much control. It's hard to react if you do get an eat. Stay in control and make big steady turns while still playing keep-away. Watch the fish for any kind of tell that it might give you. Read the fish. If it's acting interested, it is. If it starts to slow down or back off, it's time to come up with plan B.

Make the change three-dimensional. If the fish doesn't eat on the first few figure eights, it's time to make the fly do something that is different. This is where I like to also start changing the depth of the fly during the figure eight. As I bring the rod back toward me, I'll stick it deeper into the water. Often I'll push it down 4 or 5 feet. Then as I move the fly away from myself and the boat, I will bring the fly up. Now

I'm changing direction and depth at the same time. As I'm bringing the fly up, I will also speed it up a bit. It looks like it is trying to get away from the fish that is stalking it. You now have a fly that is doing three different things all at the same time. You are changing direction, changing depth, and changing speed—all trigger factors. If I'm watching a fish follow and it doesn't seem all that aggressive, I will start with this move. You never know what will get a neutral fish to flip the switch. Giving the fish something different and elusive is often the thing that will close the deal.

As I've said over and over, time on the water and experience will truly move you to the next level. After fishing for a while, you will likely come up with your own cadence and learn what works best for you when it comes to closing the deal on the figure eight. The more muskies you see and observe, the more knowledge you'll gain. Remember, no matter how many fish you see, they are still muskies. You can never be sure what reaction you'll get from them.

It's all about the close. What have you done for me lately? Muskie fly fishing is a very humbling experience most days. Increasing your close rate will go a long way in making the game something that you look forward to playing. Like any other sport that you participate in, there are two things that usually separate the good from the great: how you handle yourself under pressure, and when pressure is applied how you perform or close. All the great athletes have it—a killer instinct that no matter what is thrown at them, they are going to finish strong. They have a never-die attitude. This is what separates the good closer from the great closer.

Kip Notes

- Just as in sales, nothing will improve your closing rate like experience. Time on the water is the greatest teacher in the world.
- Strip-set, strip-set, strip-set.
- Finish every cast.
- Learn to read fish.
- Learn to work your flies, and use flies that move after the movement.
- Make your fly movement three-dimensional: speed, direction, and depth.

CHAPTER SEVEN

THE SEASONS

Seasonal activity can be one of the most important factors in muskie fishing. Knowing muskies' seasonal movements is key to locating them. If you're casting your fly over water that isn't very likely to hold muskies, you're spinning your wheels. Now, the old saying "Even a blind squirrel can find a nut" may be true, but it's just not very smart fishing. I'm a big believer in putting a plan together for your day or days on the water, and seasonality plays a big part in a game plan. Having a good idea where the fish are holding and what kind of mood they're in is key to stacking the poker chips in your favor.

We'll talk more in the next chapter about other factors that can help put more chips in your pile. For the purposes of this chapter, we're looking at the big picture. Once you have fished your body of water for a while, the seasonal movements will become clearer and clearer. If you go to your fishing spot on July 15, those years of experience fishing your water in mid-July will most likely tell you where to begin. Once again, this is time on the water. Experience will point you in the right direction, and then it is up to you to start putting the pieces together. Most experienced muskie guides have their bodies of water patterned as thoroughly as they can. They know that if a certain situation is happening, the muskies should be here.

I got a great piece of advice when I first started guiding: Write things down. Did I take this advice? No. It is a big regret of mine. Now, every year is different, but by having my observations written down on paper I could have referenced them and made my job a lot easier. I was lazy. I didn't want to take the time after a long day on the water to write anything down. I had a boat to clean, lunches to prepare, flies to tie, equipment to go over, and my family. I didn't want to take that extra ten minutes and write down something that could have saved me hours of frustration three years from then. Another thing I wish I would have written down are the thousands of stories that I have heard and been a part of over the years. If you're really going to get serious about chasing muskies, I would encourage you to start a log and write your observations down. Good and bad. They are all part of the

Fall is both beautiful and a prime time for chasing muskies in many locations.
AARON OTTO

puzzle and can help when you can't find that last missing piece. If you really want to get muskies dialed in, it helps immensely to have years of data to look back on. Start taking notes. It doesn't have to be much, just the basics. Things like date, time, weather, water temps, weed growth, pressure, presentations, and flies used can all be of great use as you start to stockpile your data. This only has to take a few minutes and can be worth its weight in gold. Any scientist will tell you that your study is only as good as the data you have to support it. Make taking notes part of your day on the water. You'll be glad you did.

There are three seasons that muskie anglers should concern themselves with: post-spawn/early summer, summer, and fall/winter. Those seasons can be even broken down more, but for the sake of this book, we'll try to keep it somewhat simple. I'm writing about what I know. I will use the seasons here in the Upper Midwest as a reference. In the South we all know that the seasons are longer and can be very different from those here in Minnesota. I would just adjust your muskie calendar to where you'll be fishing. Post-spawn where you fish might be April. Here in the Upper Midwest, it is most likely late May in a typical year. Everything that I reference is also a typical seasonal cycle. We all know how different each year can be. These will be generalities, and it will be up to you to put the pieces together. Time on the water will bring it all into focus a lot better than I can describe on paper.

Remember that as with all seasonal cycles, you have to always be thinking about the biology of the fish. As we discussed in chapter 2, there are four things that a muskie is most concerned about: making more muskies, finding food sources, staying comfortable, and not working hard. These four factors go hand in hand with seasonality movements. When you overlap the four basic needs of muskies with the seasons of the year, you are on your way to patterning them. The more precise your pattern on the waters that you fish, the more your odds will increase. Any guide that is worth his or her salt survives on knowing these patterns. It is the key to their success. Muskies can be easily patterned if it is approached with diligence and patience.

POST-SPAWN / LATE SPRING

Here in the Upper Midwest, this usually is anywhere from the middle of May till the end of June. Once again, this will vary greatly depending on what kind of spring we have. It's pretty simple. If it's a warm spring, you just move everything up. If it's a cold and wet spring, push the spawn back. Like I said, it's all related to water temperatures.

In the Upper Midwest the fishing season doesn't generally start until after the spawn. Most states try to protect spawning fish so that they can do their thing in peace. This helps ensure that our naturally spawning populations remain strong and that the fishery continues to grow and flourish. One word about spawning fish: Not all states have these regulations in place. If your state lets you fish for muskies during the spawning period, *don't*. Leave the fish be. I shouldn't even have to bring this subject up, but as a responsible angler you owe it to the resource to give them the best chance to have a successful spawn. Spawning fish are easy to spot. They're in very shallow water, and if caught or even harassed, it can have a very adverse effect on spawning success. Just leave them be and let them make more muskies so everyone is happy.

This period of the year is that of rapid transformation. Everything is happening quickly as far as seasons go. You have fish moving into their spawning areas to spawn. This is only a brief time in the grand scheme of the year. Immediately after the spawn takes place, the exit from their spawning areas into their summer migration route begins. This transition time can make finding the fish difficult. At no other time of the year does the seasonal transformation take place in such a short amount of time. If you can put the pieces of the puzzle together during this time, the fishing can be very good. Post-spawn fish are hungry and looking to eat.

Here in Minnesota, fishing generally opens the first Saturday of June. Spawn has usually wrapped up, leaving us with post-spawn conditions or early summer conditions depending on how warm the spring was. It is also opening weekend, so you have very little, if any, intel to point you in the right direction as to where the fish are located. We know that the fish have spawned and will be looking for food to rebuild their strength after the rigors of the spawn. This time of year, I play the inside-out

EARLY SUMMER ON THE JAMES
RIVER IS HARD TO BEAT.
JON LUKE

game. This means that I start in shallow water near spawning grounds and then work out from there into deeper water and likely holding areas.

Rivers and lakes are very different when it comes to locating fish. I start looking in the spawning areas for some holdover fish. The big females will deposit their eggs and hit the road for the most part. I start in the spawning areas because you never know. You know that they were there at one time in the last few weeks. It's a starting point. Every lake or river system is different. In some waters they spawn in only a few inches of water, while in others they might spawn in much deeper water. Know your watershed as best you can and figure that out as soon as you can. If you don't find fish shallow, it's time to make a move and begin looking a bit deeper. It's early and we are just trying to locate some muskies.

In a lake the second spot I'm going to look is the first hard break or first established weed line out from the spawning area. If it is a cold spring with very little early weed growth, look to that break. Muskies will often move out of their spawning area to set up on an area that has food and comfort. Remember, they are pretty wiped out and need to be by a preferred food source. If the spring was cool, that warmer water near the spawning area also gives them comfort. If you don't move anything after a while, it can get pretty tough. The trick to post-spawn fish is to cover a lot of water. When the season first opens up, you are just looking to find some fish to see where they might be. With the fly rod it is just that much harder to cover as much water as a conventional gear angler can.

The third place I would consider is the main lake basin. Muskies will often spawn and head straight to the big open water of the main basin. They are safe there and large schools of food are available to eat at a moment's notice. Think of it as a bit like saltwater fishing bait balls in the summer. They just follow these groups of bait and eat when they want. The only problem with muskies is that there just aren't a lot of them and finding them with a fly rod can be a daunting task. You might have thousands of acres of water containing these fish, and you are very limited with the fly rod. Conventional gear anglers are often trolling these main lake basins, covering a vast amount of water looking for the lone wolfs that are cruising these areas. They're using their electronics to locate the schools of bait, and with the bait there are fish close by. If you have access to good electronics, it might be best to drive around and try to locate some bait. Electronics are amazing and will only get better with advancing technology. I would think long and hard about chasing main-lake fish with a fly rod without electronics this time of year. It takes a special angler to cast blindly all day in the middle of a lake. Discipline is the biggest asset you can have when approaching these fish. It's grueling but the payoff can be a fish of a lifetime.

In a river situation, you should look in quiet water that has some weed growth coming up and gives the fish easy access to food. You can often find muskies laid up in these flats, soaking up the sun and resting. These areas can be the same as spawning areas or very close to them. Muskies are never far from a food source during this time of year. The rivers at this time are usually teeming with likely meals. The muskies are often in a neutral mood, but never leave fish to find fish.

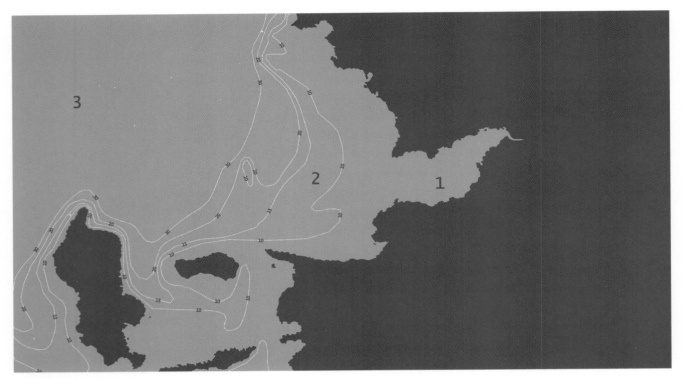

Some spring spots
KIP VIETH

This is one time during the year that you can sometimes sight-fish for muskies. Remember, generally speaking, rivers are not as deep as lakes and the fish are often holding in shallower water than in a lake. A deep hole in rivers in the Upper Midwest is 10 feet deep. Those deep holes can also have a good amount of current and aren't the most comfortable spot in the river during this time of year. In the spring the baitfish are also moving into shallower water to spawn. Everything in the river during the spring is looking for shallower water. Muskies follow food, and this will keep them shallow in a river longer than in a lake, often because they don't have any other options.

I often will look for incoming streams that are pushing food out into the main river. Baitfish will often run up these streams to spawn and then return to the main river after the spawn. A hungry muskie is often waiting for their return to make an easy meal out of them. Look for that first drop where the creek dumps in and slower current adjacent to the incoming stream. Creek mouths are always a good spot to look no matter what time of year you're fishing. They hold bait year-round, offer cooler temps in the heat of summer, and make for good ambush spots with deeper holding water in the fall. Creek mouths can be a recipe for success throughout the year. Never overlook them. Even in lakes, feeder streams offer the same advantages.

As the water warms and the days move into the summer months, things begin to settle down. Muskies find their summer haunts, and there is a little less guesswork during these months. They're still muskies and will always be a challenge, but the transition phase of the spring/summer is over. Things have settled down, and summer is upon the angler.

A fine summertime muskie taken on the James River
JON LUKE

SUMMER

Summer is often looked upon as one of the best times of the year to fish for muskies. The weeds are growing and water temperatures are rising, and with those rising temperatures the muskie's metabolism is also rising. The warmer water means that a muskie has to eat to keep its fuel tank full due to its higher metabolism rate in the warmer water. All of this points to more consistent fishing and hopefully a higher muskie contact rate.

The warmer weather also brings other things that aren't always best for muskie fishing. Traffic on the water increases, as does fishing pressure. It's vacation season, and anglers and other people are taking in as much of the summer as they can. This is especially true here in the Upper Midwest, where long winters can wear at an angler's soul. In the summertime the only place most hearty Midwesterners want to be is outside, often on the water. Every season has its challenges, and you have to learn how to deal with them if you want to become a good muskie angler.

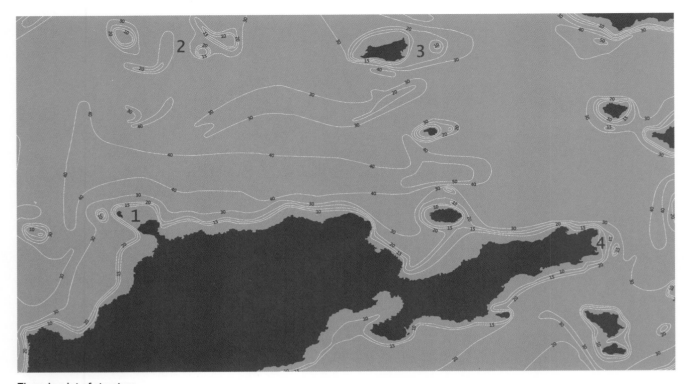

There is a lot of structure during the dog days of summer. Time on the water will reveal active fish.

MINNESOTA DEPARTMENT OF NATURAL RESOURCES, REPRINTED WITH PERMISSION

During the summer months, muskie fishing can turn into a numbers game. As we touched upon in the post-spawn section, often it's about covering a lot of water to find the active fish. The goal for the summer is to put your fly by as many fish as you can. Remember, these fish can be highly active due to the warming water and really feeling the need to eat. The fly, as we mentioned, can be a little limiting here. The fly fisher just can't cover as much water as a conventional angler can. You need to pick your areas of higher productivity and work them. If you tried to cover all of the possible holding spots, you'd wear out in a hurry. The muskie fly angler needs to dial in their spots and work them smarter than the average angler.

So, what are good summer spots? That's a loaded question. As I have said many times in this book, every lake is different. A lake that sees a limited amount of pressure can be totally different from a lake that is a popular muskie fishery. Having a good idea where to begin never hurts, but really learning your fishery will go a long way. We'll look at a few spots below, but remember these are just generalizations.

Rocky points and bars with deep water close by are always a good place to start. Saddles are areas that lie between two rock bars, and fish often cruise these areas because they act a little like a funnel. They also provide two rocky areas that the fish can hunt, depending on wind and other factors. Look for emerging weed flats in the early part of the summer, and established weed lines in the later part. Also, don't overlook large weed beds. They are tough to fish, but they do hold muskies. These are all great places to look. They all have one thing in common, and that is they hold baitfish. They also give the muskies a place to hide and to escape to if they get uncomfortable. If I'm looking at a new lake or other body of water, these are some of the first types of structure that I look for.

Today's electronics and mapping capabilities certainly remove a lot of the guess-work. If you're looking to go old-school, however, there are still lake maps available. Many of these will highlight possible productive spots for you. Several Midwest states have these types of publications focusing on their waters, and most state DNR web-sites also provide some kind of guidance when it comes to a particular body of water. Even better than that is actually talking to the state fisheries biologist that manages the particular body of water that you are interested in. They are a wealth of informa-tion and are often the first call I make when I'm looking into a new body of water.

To give you a better sense of what I'm talking about, let's look at a lake map. This map was pulled from a DNR website. As I mentioned, the local DNR is often my first stop when I'm doing my research. This is a great tool and gives the angler a good overview of the body of water under consideration. You can look at a lake from the comfort of your home and then use the electronics in your boat to pinpoint these spots. Following is just a small sample of areas to look for. I chose this particular lake because it has so much structure.

#1 has just about everything that a muskie angler is looking for in the summer months, starting with a large rock bar and flat with a steep drop-off next to it. To the west of the bar is a small island that forms a wonderful saddle area. Depending on time of year, weeds will most likely be found in and around the structure. An angler could spend hours exploring every nook and cranny of this one spot alone.

#2 is a classic mid-lake basin set of bars. This one has a classic saddle between the two bars and a large flat off the east bar to explore. As I look at this spot on a laptop without ever having fished it, it says large fish to me. It's a little off the beaten path and in the middle of a large basin. A perfect spot for a large fish to call home.

#3 is an island that is also out in the middle of the basin. It has a nice gradient drop to it and a flat and saddle on the east side.

#4 is another classic point with saddle areas and great ambush spots all around it.

These are just a few spots but will give you a general idea of what to look for. What a map doesn't show are the weed lines and beds that might be near these areas. The only way to really find quality weed structure is to get on the lake and fish it. As mentioned earlier, weeds are an important part of some muskies' habitat. A lot of muskies will make weed habitat a part of their summer homes. It can be a deep weed line next to rocks or a big weed flat. Weeds offer everything that a muskie needs to remain fat and happy. They offer cover and a large food supply close by. The fish don't have to expend much energy to feed due to the amount of food that also calls weeds home.

Weeds are probably also the best cover on the lake. As the summer drags on, the weeds just get thicker and thicker, making the muskies all but impossible to get at. Only a couple things can push the muskies out of these spots, and they are water temperatures and fishing pressure. Muskies will move out of the warmer water as they begin to get stressed by the higher water temps. They will search out more comfort-able water, and this often involves going deeper into the water column. Keep an eye on water temperatures, and this will often point you in the right areas to fish. If the muskies have been relating to weeds most of the year, they probably will continue to

A summer-season beast
MARK OLSON

do so. They are nothing if not a creature of habit. They'll probably set up on a deeper weed line that offers cooler temperatures, while still providing cover and food.

One good thing about weeds is that they set up very nicely for the fly angler. It often involves concentrating your efforts on smaller areas. The fly rod is perfect for this type of fishing. Working a weed line or a flat can be done very effectively with a fly rod. Pockets on a large weed flat can also be very productive and are great areas to work a topwater presentation. Dropping your fly into a weed pocket and making that topwater presentation as loud as you can will often get the fish looking up for that easy meal. This is where the fly angler might have an advantage over the conventional angler. Working the slop weeds in the summer can be done with a lit-tle more precision with a fly. And remember, you don't have to reel your line in to make another cast. Simply pick up your fly off the water and hit the next spot. You can cover a lot of weeds in a relatively easy and efficient way. Another reason to fish this slop is that these fish are relatively unpressured. Most conventional anglers just get frustrated with all the weeds and will move on. This is where the persistent fly angler can make hay.

Another method is to follow a deep weed line and work the edge. Position yourself off the weed line, casting right at the edge of it and working your fly out from the edge. Topwater is always a good option here also. I will often run it with a standard subsurface fly and then go back a little later and run it with a topwater presentation, or vice versa.

Don't be afraid of the weeds. They can seem like a real obstacle at times and they often are, but they hold fish if the conditions are right. Don't overlook them just because they look daunting. If it looks

A beautiful summer-season river in the Upper Midwest
KIP VIETH

daunting, let me tell you, other anglers see the same thing. Let's face it: Most of us are lazy and not willing to put in the work in those areas. We'll talk about fishing pressure a lot in the next chapter. It's a big factor in muskie fishing, especially on popular waters. You're doing something different that most anglers aren't willing or able to do. That extra work can really pay off. It's always good to approach things a little differently at times on waters that see a lot of pressure.

River situations are really no different than lakes. There is one big difference, though: The fish can't go deeper to escape warmer water. Rivers run a pretty steady temperature from top to bottom. There may be slight temperature differences, but nothing that is going to make that big of a difference. Muskies in rivers are looking for three main things during the hot summer months: food, optimal temperatures, and well-oxygenated water. You can often find muskies in very shallow riffles and runs during this season. Suckers love to be in the riffles during the summer, and the muskies are often not far behind. I have seen muskies chasing suckers in about 6 inches of water at times. It is a pretty amazing spectacle to behold.

If there is a spring or a coldwater feeder creek anywhere near this habitat, you have probably found a summer home for some muskies. It has everything that they could possiblely need: food, oxygen, and cool water. They can sometimes be very concentrated on these cool water sources. The muskie's metabolism is going full throttle with the warmer water temperatures. Not only do they need a good amount of food, they also need oxygen. The riffles, springs, and feeder creeks provide a great source of oxygen-rich water. They need that oxygen-rich water to keep the fire burning. It's just like an actual fire—without the proper amount of oxygen, it just doesn't burn. A muskie needs that oxygen to keep it fueled and healthy.

If you have a series of springs and deeper water nearby, that is also a great spot to look. Springs will add the oxygen, and the deeper water provides cover that muskies prefer. There will likely be a good food source nearby with the springwater being

Battling both the elements
and the fish in the late season
is a common theme.
KIP VIETH

introduced into the system. Like I've said, muskies can be patterned relatively easily if you know the water you are fishing and a little about the fish's biology.

The late summer sets up the early fall fishing. Just like the spring, the early fall is a transition period. The one advantage that you have over the spring is that you have been fishing and have an idea where the fish are and what they are doing. This is the time of year when observation is key. Muskies can be on a spot one day and out the next. Keeping tabs on your prey is key during this transition time.

FALL

The days begin to get shorter and shorter. Weeds begin to die off. Water temperatures begin to fall, and the sun is lower on the horizon. These are all contributing factors that trigger a muskie into its fall transition. If you keep a fishing diary, this is a great time to reference what the muskies have done in past years. If you don't keep one, this is a great reason to start. Gathering that data will help during these transition times. Looking at your past experiences on the water can help you stay in the game during this transition

You might ask, "How will I know when muskies are starting their transition?" The answer: "The water where you fished last week and moved three fish is now empty." It is really that simple. They have moved, and it is now that the game begins. It's really kind of like hide-and-seek. You know they can't be too far. It's just a matter of finding their new haunt. There is only one thing that really makes muskies move and that is the food supply. The cooler water has also made them more comfortable. They are in a much better mood than they were when the water temperatures were overly warm. I like to use this analogy: How hungry are you when it is 90 degrees outside? There is a reason Thanksgiving is in November, and it's not to celebrate the harvest. It's because people just didn't want to eat that much food any other time of the year.

Look for areas that concentrate bait and offer a pinch point.
RUSS GRONTAREK

If we get a strong cold snap in late summer, it is often a trigger that will charge the muskies up. It's like someone turned the AC on and they get some well-deserved relief from the heat. This can happen well before the fall transition some years. I have been out smallmouth fishing when a cold snap hits. It's often in late August, well before one would be looking for transitional fish. The muskies seem to be smashing bait all over. The smallmouth fishing stinks, but the muskie bite can be very good. It's as if they have all this pent-up energy from those long warm days. As soon as it cools, all that energy is released and they begin to go on a frenzy. Keep an eye on the weather forecast this time of year. It can pay off in a big way.

Bridges usually offer pinch points and deeper holding water during the late season.
RUSS GRONTAREK

As the bait starts to migrate, the muskies will not be too far behind. Many of the shallow weed beds start to die off as the water temperatures fall. The baitfish have to find a more hospitable area to call home. Baitfish that called the weed beds home in summer, like bluegills and perch, will head to deeper weed lines as the shallow ones die off. They are looking for any cover that they can find. They don't want to become Mr. Muskie's next meal. Mr. Muskie knows this and will be waiting for an unsuspecting victim. In the fall, all we are trying to do is intercept the bait as they make their transitions. Muskies are following schools of bait. If we can beat them to the punch, we stack the odds a bit more in our

Dams are a late-season hot spot. They are a barrier where bait and muskies concentrate.
RUSS GRONTAREK

Current breaks offer great holding and ambush areas for muskies.
RUSS GRONTAREK

favor. Watching for the signs and knowing your body of water is paramount when it comes to putting together a pattern, no matter what time of year. A good source if you have questions about the baitfish that live in your home water is your local DNR biologist. He or she can provide you with a lot of answers to seasonal movements and possible spawning areas for the different baitfish in your body of water.

One of the best places to look for fish in the fall are pinch points. Another great area to look at are dams. This type of water concentrates both fish and bait and can be very productive. They are easy to find, and for a beginner fly angler these are great spots to begin to look for fish. There is in most cases deeper holding water near these areas that a muskie can winter in and remain fat and happy. There is also usually some kind of current involved in these areas. The current can help the angler locate the fish a little easier. The fish will set up on these current seams and wait for baitfish to come by for an easy meal.

Some baitfish spawn in the fall and begin to concentrate and move to their spawning areas. On the bigger waters here in Minnesota, this is one of the best times to be on the water. If you find the baitfish's spawning area, you can bet there are several large muskies in the area. Northern ciscoes—or as we call them in Minnesota, tullibees—spawn in the fall in rocky reefs in shallower water. They're a larger baitfish that have a high fat content and make a perfect meal for a muskie that is stocking up for the long winter. Regular ciscoes spawn in shallow, gravelly bays. This spawning activity happens later in the fall, but it is a great example of following the food source. In the fall, that is the name of the game. Muskies are eating at a rapid clip and there has to be food nearby.

A river is really not that much different from a lake in the fall. We are still playing the game of follow the bait. The main bait in my area are suckers. As the water temperature drops, they have to move also. The riffles that the suckers called home in the summer have changed. They were an amazing food source all summer, but the cooler water has slowed the food supply and is forcing the suckers to abandon these once-fruitful riffles for slower and deeper water. Simply put, they are moving to their wintering holes. This also causes baitfish to concentrate, just like on a lake.

The cooler water temperatures have also negated the need for the springs with their higher oxygen content. They're no longer needed to ensure the muskie's survival. The deep holes and flats adjacent to them are home to most of the bait during the winter. As the baitfish migrate to these holes, the muskies follow. The deeper water protects all the fish from the brutal winter that will soon arrive. The muskies like to set up on the current seams and deep wood that are near these wintering holes. Muskies want to preserve as much energy as they can. The slower water and protected ambush spots are the places to begin looking.

The image above is a good example. The current comes into the bank, making a deep run. You can see the rock bar that comes off of the bank pushing the current back out to the middle of the river. This makes a dead spot (marked with a star) with a current seam next to it. Nothing says *muskie* in the fall more than a spot like this. There is an ample amount of food close by and a deep, slow water trough. This is a spot that a muskie can call home all fall and winter long. To imagine a smaller version of this, just replace the rock bar with a tree or some kind of logjam and you have the same effect. Deepwater ambush spots near seams are where the majority of our fish come from in the fall and early winter here in the Upper Midwest.

Knowing the biology of muskies and their food sources is key to progressing through the fishing season. Keep notes, and become a student of the fish and the body of water that you're fishing. I have said it over and over again: Muskie fishing is hard work. Not just on the water, but in the mental game as well. Learning and soaking up as much information as you can will make patterning muskies on your body of water that much easier. I think I end almost every chapter by saying this, but it all boils down to time spent on the water. Learning your quarry's movements takes time and study. The more you do it, the more confident you will become.

Kip Notes

- Put time in on the water.
- Use the muskie's biology to your advantage.
- Muskies are patternable and predictable. Learn the patterns and the seasonality of the muskie and your odds will increase dramatically.
- Follow the bait and you'll find the fish. Learn what forage the muskies prefer in a particular part of the season on the system you are fishing.
- Stay alert of your surroundings.

CHAPTER EIGHT

FACTORS IN THE HUNT: THE TRIGGERS

"What are we doing?" asked a client as I pushed the drift boat down the river. "We're heading down to that wood pile downriver where I know there is a nice fish for the moonrise," I answered. "Is it really that big of a deal?" she asked. "It can be," I said firmly.

I have to admit that when I first started chasing muskies on the fly, I thought that the moon phase factor was hogwash. I knew that weather certainly had a huge effect on angling success—it doesn't take an angler long to figure that out. A trout angler will tell you that cloudy days are, for the most part, better for fishing than a high blue-bird sky. The fish are just a bit happier on those cloudy days and more willing to eat. Now, we all know that there are exceptions to every rule. Caddis like sunny days, and if there is a good hatch, things can change dramatically. It's all about being observant and knowing, as best you can, what is happening around you.

Moon phases are a different story. Unless you track the moon activity, it's hard to know just what is going on and when events are happening. I used to give my buddies a lot of grief about the moon. I thought it was just an excuse for not catching fish. They'd tell me that the moon was a little off and that would explain the fish being off. I'd look at them and just roll my eyes. Then I got more serious about the game and started to read and ask a lot of questions. I started noticing things. Yes, there was something to this moon thing. Fish definitely reacted differently at certain times of the moon phase. I started paying attention and tracking it, and it soon became very clear that the moon does play a role in fish activity.

There is no doubt that muskies have a switch. When it flips, they are going to eat. I'll be on a trip and move three fish at 2:00 p.m. and draw blanks the rest of the day. I'll call my guide buddies and ask how their day went, and it will be the same story. All of their fish were moved at or around 2:00 p.m. Whatever that event was, it made

A wonderful river muskie that ate during a major moon phase

KIP VIETH

the fish decide to eat. I think the best stories that prove this are those told by tournament anglers. These are some of the best muskie anglers in the country. All tournaments are catch-and-release, and they use judge boats to verify the size and numbers of fish caught. When an angler catches a muskie, they radio to a judge boat to come and verify their fish. It can be hours of no to very few fish on the radio. Then, for whatever reason, the radio starts to fire off and the fish are being caught. This event might go on for fifteen minutes to an hour or better. Then, after the event, the radio returns to quiet.

So, what are the factors that contribute to these events? What triggers them? It can be one or a combination of trigger factors. This is where observation and fishing notes can play a very big part in putting the pieces of the puzzle together. Remember, this puzzle is like one you buy at a thrift store: There always seems to be a few pieces missing. The job of the angler is to try to put the pieces together as best they can regardless of how many pieces are missing.

I often explain to my clients that muskie fishing is just a giant poker game. The object is to stack as many chips in your favor to make the payoff that much better. Weather, moon phases, and fishing pressure are all part of the game. Having these factors in your favor can often mean the difference between cashing in big time or going home broke and busted. Trying to figure out when that big eating event will happen is all part of the game. I think it is one of the things that draws me to muskie more than anything these days. Trying to figure out when it will happen. It's always a mystery, and solving it is one of the most satisfying parts of muskie fishing to me. It doesn't happen often, but when it does, it's very rewarding.

Putting together these pieces is not that hard. Keeping an eye on what is going on with the weather, moon, and body of water that you're fishing can be the key to success. The longer you chase muskies, the more keenly you will watch for the trigger factors. Stacking these factors can increase your odds substantially. Ask any poker player and they'll tell you, give me better odds every time and I'll come out ahead more often than not.

WEATHER

I think it is a safe assumption that weather is by far the biggest factor in any angler's fishing success. I have people ask, "When is the best time to come up fishing?" Depending on the species they are chasing, it can be a totally different time of year. I like trout in the spring, smallmouth in the summer, and muskie in the fall. That's not to say you can't catch those species other times of the year, but that is usually my standard answer. The one thing that any time of year has in common with the others is the weather. If a future client asks me that question, I tell them to book their day for the best time of year for that species and pray for good weather.

Here is a perfect example. I have a big group from Kansas City that comes to smallmouth fish every year in mid-August. This is prime time for river smallmouth here in Minnesota. It's hard to beat the dog days of summer for smallmouth. Well, a few years back, the temperature dropped 20 degrees overnight and sent the fishing into a tailspin. They booked one of the best times of year for fishing, and the weather still got them. Same thing has happened on muskie trips. I guide on my buddy Bob White's Musky Madness trip every year. A few years back, the weather was absolutely beautiful— temperatures in the 90s, no wind, and sunny as all get out. Well, that's fine in mid-August, but at the end of September it can really mess up the muskie fishing.

If you're traveling a good distance for a fishing trip, there isn't much you can do but plan for the best time of year. You plan your trip, and as I said, you just pray for good weather and conditions. What I mean by "good weather" isn't necessarily good weather. You want the best weather for that species. For muskies and most other fish, a high bluebird sky with high pressure usually doesn't make for the best fishing conditions.

So, what are the best conditions for chasing muskies? I know this is a cliché, but it is whenever you have a chance to go. If you waited for what most people would consider perfect conditions, you'd probably get out a handful of times a year. The more I guide, the less I really look at every condition. Now, I know you might think that is being a poor guide, but let's look at it from a guide's perspective. I'm booked every day from the middle of May until the beginning of November. If something

Weather is one of the biggest factors influencing muskies' behavior.
AARON OTTO

isn't perfect, I don't have a choice. My clients are coming fishing and I need to give them the best day possible no matter what is going on. This doesn't mean I don't look at the weather, water flows, moon phases, and other factors that might affect our day. It means that I'm fishing no matter what, and if the water temperature falls 10 degrees, there's not a whole lot I can do about it. We're still going to be out there fishing. This is why full-time fishing guides tend to be good. They are out there every day fishing and trying to put their clients on fish regardless of what the conditions are. Any guide that has been at it for a while has seen pretty much everything and draws from those experiences. The same can be said for professional anglers and the hardest of the hard cores. Like I have said repeatedly, there is no substitute for time spent on the water.

That being said, there is one thing that will grab my attention above everything else. That is change. Nothing triggers muskies to eat more than a weather change. This is by far the biggest poker chip that you can have. It can also adversely affect the fishing more than any other factor. Remember, the switch flips both ways. What triggered the fish to eat today might shut them down tomorrow. Fishing guides probably complain more about the weather than any other human beings out there, and that includes farmers. It's too hot, too cold, too sunny, too cloudy, too windy, or any number of other excuses that we can throw in there. The only thing that you won't hear a fly-fishing guide complain about is that it is too calm.

One of the first things I ask myself every morning prior to a trip is what has changed from the day before. What's the temperature? Wind direction and speed? Barometric pressure? Current? And I always check the radar. Once I have determined what has changed, if anything, the more important question is whether there is going to be a change when I'm on the water. Is there a front coming in? Is the wind going to change direction? Anything that might upset the apple cart in either a good or bad way.

I remember as a kid, my father had a fisherman's barometer hanging in the garage. The barometer was marked when the best fishing might be taking place. I kind of wish that I had an electronic version of it. It would be set so that when the barometer started falling, it would sound an alarm. I bet there is something like that available somewhere on the internet. When the barometer starts falling and a front is coming in, I would be on high alert. The hard-core angler is watching for this situation to take place and will drop everything when it presents itself and head to their favorite water.

So, let's run through a perfect scenario. It is midsummer and the weather has been stable for about a week. A cold front is approaching, and the barometer is going to start falling throughout the day. Remember, change is the trigger, and there is no bigger change than a cold front rolling through after a week of stable weather. This is go-time. You need to get on the water and fish your "go-to spot" for that time of year. It can be spring, summer, or fall—you need to take advantage of this change. I will say this: In the summer the effect of a front seems to be a bit stronger than that in the spring or fall. Those big thunderstorms that roll through in midsummer can really get the muskies triggered.

Now, here in the Upper Midwest, we can have a front roll through every four or five days. This change still has a trigger effect, but it seems to be a little less than one that takes place when the weather has been stable for a longer period of time. The poker chip isn't worth as much, but it's still a chip in your favor and you have to be ready to play it.

The weather that separates the men from the boys is the day after that cold front and the bluebird high-pressure days that usually follow it. I always say that the fish are experiencing a high-pressure headache. It's just like us trying to function when we're not at our best. We get the job done, but it takes a little more effort and we're usually not too happy about it. The fish are the same way. As the front continues, things start to settle down and the fish get a little used to it. The high pressure usually pushes the fish tighter to cover again. It's like humans: If we aren't feeling that great, we'd rather stay in bed or chill on the couch. If someone was kind enough to deliver a pizza bedside, though, we'd most likely take a bite. This is when the angler is tested and what is meant when anglers say they're grinding. You have to have the discipline to stay in the hunt and try to put that pizza in front of one of those fish that just might take a bite. This is where time on the water can pay big dividends—learning how to read fish and how the angler can get them to trigger up and strike. A lot of these fish are followers and not really committed to eating. Using the pizza metaphor again, you need to find out if the fish likes a cheese or a supreme pizza and what it's going to take to make it grab a slice and go.

A muskie caught on a perfect fall day: cloudy, cold, and a chance of snow
KIP VIETH

I was at a high school sporting event one time and saw one of the athletes wearing a T-shirt with a saying that has stuck with me and sums up a lot of things in life: "Hard work beats talent when talent doesn't work hard." Work hard on the not-so-great days and you'll eventually be rewarded.

Weather is the most important factor in triggering a muskie to eat. Staying alert, watching your surroundings, and paying attention to frontal situations, wind directions, and temperature can have a big impact on an angler's success. It's something to study, and when you do, your success will be rewarded.

MOON PHASES

Do the moon and sun really have that big of an effect on fishing? Just ask any saltwater guide or angler that has ever climbed in a boat and explored the salt. Yes, but this is freshwater—how can it matter here in the Upper Midwest? Well, it does. I said that weather is the biggest factor in triggering muskies to eat, and it is. The only problem with the weather, as we all know, is predicting it. Moon phases and sunrises/sunsets are known a hundred years in advance. We know when they will happen and can plan our day around them, years in advance if need be. I have clients looking at next year's moon phases when they book that year's guide dates. It is the one factor that we can somewhat take advantage of.

More and more studies are being done on the effect of the moon on muskie angling. There is also plenty of anecdotal evidence that proves that the moon has a role to play in when muskies are more apt to trigger and eat. As I mentioned earlier, I used to think that the moon phase theory was hogwash. I just couldn't believe that the moon could play that big of a role in a lake or river here in Minnesota. It just seemed like another excuse for a muskie angler. As I got more into muskie fishing, I could no longer ignore what was staring me right in the face. There definitely was a correlation between moon activity and muskie activity.

If you are as old as I am, you might remember the old solunar tables in the local newspaper or *Field & Stream* magazine. They told you when the fishing and hunting times were best. I never really bought into them as a younger angler and never watched them that closely. Fast-forward thirty years, and now I have an app on my phone that basically does the same thing. I check it religiously and it is part of my daily pre-trip check when I'm chasing muskies. Not only does it give me the information that I'm looking for, but it also uses my location with the phone's GPS to give me the exact time these events will be happening in the area I will be fishing that day.

So, what is the information that I'm looking for? There are four different lunar events that occur every day that a muskie angler should consider: moonrise, moonset, moon overhead, and moon underfoot. Moonrise and moonset are just that—when the moon is coming up or setting. Nothing too complicated there. Moon overhead or underfoot is pretty self-explanatory also. The moon is directly over your head or under your feet. Think of it as moon high noon and midnight, respectively. These four events are when the moon has the most effect on muskies.

Now you need to factor in the moon phase. Is it a full moon, a new moon, or something in between? You can probably deduce that full and new moon time frames have the biggest effect on muskies. This is when the moon is at its most powerful when it comes to influencing triggering events.

Here is what a typical calendar screenshot looks like on one of the apps that I use. Most apps are pretty much the same, so just find one that you like best.

This is the monthly calendar. As you can see, the days with the strongest lunar influence have the most stars on them. These are, of course, around the new and full moon phases. If I can only fish a few days a month, I'm going to try to plan my trips around these lunar peaks. There is that much of an advantage to fishing these peaks. People often ask me what days are the best. I will say that depending on where you live and fish, there can be a big difference. We'll touch on that a bit later. Here in the Upper Midwest, particularly Minnesota, I use a party analogy. I say that the anticipation of the party is often better than the actual party. So, let's look at the calendar again. The new moon

KIP VIETH

KIP VIETH

is on October 17. You can see that the 14th through the 16th are also three-star days. I like them a bit more than the actual lunar event. I'd fish all five three-star days, but those first three can be a bit better in my opinion.

Now that we know what days to fish, let's look at the key times for the first three-star day. Remember, the best time to fish is when you can. Here is what October 14, 2020, looks like.

You can see right away that this is the start of one of the best periods of the month to fish. This is due to the new moon and strong lunar activity. It is three days before the new moon. In this screenshot you can also see sunrise and sunset, which can be very helpful too. The first thing I look at, however, is moonrise and moonset. The moon rises at 3:19 a.m. and sets at 4:55 p.m. Those are the first two times that I'm going to consider. I probably won't be fishing at 3:19 a.m., but the moonset of 4:55 p.m. is definitely in play.

The next two things that I look at is moon underfoot or overhead. In most solunar tables, these are what they consider the majors, or when they think the bite window is going to be most active. The majors on this solunar table start and end an hour and a half on each side of the lunar event. We see the zenith is 10:16 a.m., which is moon overhead. This is the time right in the middle of the first major we see. The other major is from 9:07 p.m. till 12:00 a.m. This would be moon underfoot. The minors are usually the moonrise and moonset. These rotate at different times each day. Sometimes the moonrise can be at noon. You have to check often to see what the majors and minors will be for the day you're fishing. We can see two major windows from 8:46 a.m. to 11:46 a.m. and 9:07 p.m. to 12:00 a.m. The moon overhead major is definitely in play. When I'm putting together my game plan for the day, I know that I want to be fishing in an area that is holding fish at 10:16 a.m. and 4:55 p.m.

Now, I know that some of you still aren't buying into what you might consider a dog and pony show. However, there is now solid science behind the lunar factor. In a study titled "Muskie Lunacy: Does the Lunar Cycle Influence Angler Catch of Muskellunge?" (Mark R. Vinson and Ted R. Angradi, 2014), scientists looked at the lunar cycle hypothesis, and many of these questions were answered. The authors of the study looked at catch records for 341,959 muskies from North America to test the lunar effect on catch rates. Some fascinating things were learned in the study. If you like looking at studies, I would recommend reading it in full. For the sake of this book, I will just give you the highlights.

I thought that this paragraph summed up the study very well:

Given how difficult it is to catch a muskellunge, any advantage that occurs to the moon-conscious angler is noteworthy. The maximum relative effect varied among fisheries. Overall, the effect was about 5%, but was higher (15–28%) for several popular muskellunge fisheries and for night fishing. When translated to the reduction in time required to catch a musky, our findings suggest that each muskellunge will be caught 2 to 5 h sooner by lunar-phase-optimizing angler than by the angler choosing his fishing days at random. Expressed another way anglers "fish the moon," the "Fish of 10,000 Casts" becomes the fish of about 9,500 casts.

Other findings in the study were that the farther up in latitude, the bigger the effect on the fish (>48 degrees N). The lunar effect was greater on larger muskies (>40 inches). The lunar effect was stronger in midsummer than in June and October. The lunar effect was weaker in Wisconsin than in Minnesota and Ontario, and the authors hypothesized that this might be due to the smaller fish and smaller bodies of water in Wisconsin. It was a very enlightening study that brought some science to what hard-core muskie anglers have known for some time. The lunar effect is real.

SUN PHASES

The sun can play an important role as well. It is mostly the lower-light periods of rise and set that I concentrate on. Fish are, for the most part, more active during these low-light periods. The solunar tables include the sunrise and sunset, and they're there for a reason. Low light matters.

I like to be on the water during the low-light times of the day. I particularly like the sunset. I think it's the old bow hunter in me. If I was out in the morning, I knew the hunting was never going to get any better than it was right then. It was only going to get worse as the sun continued to rise. When out in the evening, I knew that the hunting would get better as the sun got lower and lower. It was easier to concentrate on my surroundings while bow hunting in the evening. I find my muskie fishing is the same way. In the evening it has always been easier to fish and more productive for me. I know it's more productive just because I'm concentrating that much harder and getting into the game a little bit more in the evening.

If you looked at it scientifically, there probably isn't much of a difference between the morning and evening low-light times. It's just one of my quirks, and if you don't have any yet, you will soon. Muskie fishing does that to an angler.

FISHING PRESSURE

You are reading this book to go muskie fishing. Like it or not, you're going to put some kind of fishing pressure on a body of water. Fishing pressure is just the amount of angler activity at any given time. Some lakes and rivers see very little in the way of fishing pressure, and some bodies of water see an amazing amount. These are usually

Low-light periods can be the most productive times of the day.
JON LUKE

the ones closer to denser population centers. No other factor that we have talked about will become a bigger factor over time than fishing pressure. The weather is going to do what it does. The sun and moon will do what they have been doing for as long as we can remember, but some angler racing you to your favorite muskie spot will be the one factor that continues to change and evolve.

Be careful what you wish for. The sport of muskie fly fishing has grown by leaps and bounds. With that growth comes pressure, like it or not. I have said over and over that the line a guide has to walk is razor thin. It's the line between making a living and supporting your family and exploiting or exposing the resources to more people than you care to. You might even cause the resource harm if you're not careful. But the kids have to eat too. I struggle with this a lot, especially while muskie fishing.

Muskies are a different fish. There just aren't a lot of them, especially big ones. Keep in mind that they are the alpha predator, not a bluegill. Biologists tell us that there is one 40-inch or better fish per 10 acres in a quality muskie lake. If you're on a 3,000-acre lake, there might be 300 muskies in it. Those 40-plus-inch fish are fairly old and have probably seen a thing or two over their lifetime. In other words, they're educated. They live in a pretty concentrated area for the most part and are very susceptible to fishing pressure. Let's face it—they didn't get that big by being stupid. Their moody disposition doesn't help much either. So, on a pressured body of water, you now have very few big fish that are smart, educated, and moody. The funniest part of the whole equation is that you are trying to fool those big fish with a bunch of deer hair and chicken feathers. Doesn't sound like it might be the easiest thing to do. The one thing about fishing pressure is that it isn't going away anytime soon.

Fishing pressure is here to stay. Now you have to ask yourself what the best way is to approach it and how you can sometimes turn it to your advantage. The first thing to remember is to be respectful. Remember, it's just fishing when all is said and done. There are always going to be people that hole shoot you, steal your spot right out from under you, and are just plain rude. The best way to handle this is to move on, ignore them, and remember that not everyone knows what proper etiquette is. I'll say this many times in this section: It's just fishing. It's supposed to be fun. Muskie fishing is frustrating enough. You don't need to add to that frustration by letting the actions of someone else dictate your day. Another benefit of moving on is that often you're forced to fish something that you normally wouldn't. You might have been overlooking a spot that holds fish just because it wasn't in your comfort zone. Being forced to explore is not always a bad thing. Keep a positive attitude, and who knows what can happen?

Don't be that angler either. If someone beats you to a spot or gets to the river before you, too bad. You lost. Get up earlier or find another body of water to fish. Don't ruin your day or another angler's day by being rude or unprofessional. Set an example for that person, and hopefully they'll return the favor. Communication goes a long way in helping these situations. I have floated behind boats a lot in my time guiding. That boat in front of me might be getting those fish active and I'm behind them cleaning up. One thing about muskie fishing, you never know what can happen. The boat in front of you might be the trigger that puts a fish in your boat. Remember, it's just fishing and there is no need to get worked up over it. It's supposed to be fun and relaxing. Do your part to make sure that it is.

A brief word on social media. I know that everyone likes to share their nice catches and adventures on the different social media outlets. I enjoy seeing what is going on out in the fly-fishing world too. I'm as guilty as the next guide of using the platform to create some buzz about my business. In today's society it is a necessary evil for the small business owner. It's all part of that razor-thin line that I mentioned earlier. Has it hurt fishing? I think it has, but it's not going away. Just use the platform responsibly and ethically. If you don't think that people are watching the feeds for spots, you're wrong. I can point to a lot of examples of anglers picking up spots from social media posts. I've done it. Back in the beginning of social media, someone who was willing to dig a little could get the GPS coordinates from a picture. For example, awhile back an angler put a picture of a 20-inch smallmouth on social media. In the picture you could see a dock. One of my friends who was pretty good with computers pulled the GPS coordinates from the picture. The next week, guess who was holding the 20-inch smallmouth in a picture? We just educated that fish a little more because someone innocently posted a nice fish on social media.

You can no longer get GPS coordinates from pictures on social media, but you can study a picture and see where that 48-inch muskie might be calling home. I've photoshopped some posts of mine to keep the landmarks out of the frame. It's pretty easy to see where a fish was caught if the Highway 32 bridge is in the background or the landing by Big Buck Island is in the post. I'm not saying don't use social media, just be careful with it. There are other anglers mining posts all the time, so don't be too upset when your spot by the bridge has two guys fishing it when you pull up next time. Don't be a part of the problem.

Fishing pressure can present a number of unique challenges. I live north of the Minneapolis–St. Paul metro area. There are nearly four million people living here, and if you know anything about Minnesota's culture, you know that a good amount of those four million fish. Minneapolis is known as the City of Lakes, and some of the best muskie waters in the state are just minutes to an hour from downtown. To say these lakes see a little fishing pressure would be an understatement. Anglers can leave their metro jobs or homes and be on a world-class muskie lake in a matter of minutes. Muskie fishing has grown by leaps and bounds in all aspects, not just fly fishing. There is pressure from all parts of the angling spectrum. I often joke that the muskies in most class 1 lakes in the metro area are born with a GPS chip in their heads. I would be willing to bet that 90 percent of the large muskies that swim in a certain very popular lake in the metro area have waypoints assigned to them.

With today's electronics, anglers are getting more and more educated, along with the fish. Muskie waypoints are commonplace in most muskie anglers' depth-finders and electronics. When a muskie is moved or seen, that spot is automatically put into the angler's database, either in their head or in their boat's electronics. Muskies, as we have discussed, are very territorial and if you have seen them once, chances are they won't be far from that spot. As long as bait and cover are close by, they aren't going too far. I bet if you compared four committed muskie anglers' databases, there would be a ton of overlap of the fish that they have marked.

Remember that large muskies are pretty rare. Let's say that Lake W has 50 big fish (>40 inches) in it. They are all marked in 150 anglers' databases for the month of August. On any given evening, of the 150 anglers, 25 are out muskie fishing a total of 4 hours. If you do the math, that is a total of 700 hours of pressure per week on just 50 large fish. If we then divide 700 by 50, each fish has seen a total of 14 hours of fishing pressure per week. That's real pressure, and it isn't too far of a stretch on popular lakes and rivers. Now, I made these numbers up, but they are a good educated guess after talking to a few guides and anglers about the pressure on these metro lakes.

These fish have seen every bucktail, Bull Dawg, or any number of hard muskie baits. Think of how many times a bait has been presented to a fish in a fourteen-hour window each week, let alone a full season. When fishing pressured waters—and most waters are pressured these days—you have to try to crack that code. One way to do it is to pay attention to the bite window factors that we talked about earlier. You would think that a fish that has seen that many baits throughout their lifetime, and most likely hooked by a few, would never eat. This is where it's all about that window. When they decide to eat, nothing is going to stop them. If you're there when the trigger is pulled, you might hit pay dirt.

Another way to try to get one of these pressured fish to eat is by presenting something that they have hardly seen before. This is where fly anglers can differentiate

With a little digging, it wouldn't be too hard to figure out where this fish was caught.
JON LUKE

themselves from the hard-tackle anglers. More and more anglers are fly fishing for muskies, but it's not anywhere near the number of conventional anglers out there. When you show a muskie something completely different, it might be enough to get it to eat. Remember, fish don't have hands, and if they want to check something out, it has to go in their mouths. Showing a fish that has just seen fourteen hours of bucktails, Medusas, and stick baits a fly might be the thing that closes the deal. It is something different, and it might be their curiosity that will do them in. Curiosity killed the cat, and it also caught a lot of muskies over the years.

The flip side can also be true. There are rivers in northern Wisconsin and Minnesota that are almost exclusively fly fishing these days. Comparatively speaking, they see very few conventional anglers. If I wanted to try to put a fish in the boat and didn't care how I did it, I would probably throw conventional muskie gear. It is something totally different. You can cover ten times the water in half the time, and it's easier to put a hook in a fish with conventional gear. I'm trying to show them something completely different, and sometimes a bucktail is very different. If I'm fishing a watershed that has a lot of fly-fishing pressure, I'm going to shake my flies and fishing up and give them something a bit different. I might go to a bigger fly or smaller fly, one with a long tail on it, strip it differently, a different color—it really doesn't matter. I'm just trying to find something to get that fish to put that fly in its mouth.

Fishing pressure is a serious factor when you are out chasing muskies on water that sees a lot of anglers. You can sit and lament about it as much as you want, but it really isn't going to change anything. One of my fishing partners looked at me as I was barking about all the pressure we were seeing one day, and said with a scowl, "Dude, learn to deal with it and shut up. Let's fish." It's some of the best advice I ever got, and I did deal with it. There are certain rivers that I try to avoid simply because it's not worth the hassle. Sometimes it's just easier to do that. Don't let someone else's attitude dictate yours. That same friend's son used to say to him, "Don't hate, congratulate." It's just fishing. It's supposed to be fun, remember?

FACTORING THE FACTORS

Factors that might play a role in triggering an eat—that's what this chapter is all about. The factors that can help or hurt a muskie angler in their pursuit of muskies. What we are looking at is how to recognize these factors and incorporate them into our game plan for the day. You have probably realized that there are factors within these factors. Weather, moon, sun, and fishing pressure all play a role in our success as muskie anglers. Let's look at how you can plan your fishing trip to take these factors into account and turn them in your favor to give you the best chance of success.

The first factors that an angler should consider are the ones that they can control. Lunar and sun factors are really the only things that we can count on. You want to know what moon phase will be taking place during your fishing trip. Is it going to be a new moon, a full moon, or a period in between? If I can plan my fishing day during one of the strong lunar periods, I certainly will. Look at the monthly solunar tables and figure out what days have the strongest effect. The next thing to check are the major and minor feeding times for the day or days that you'll be fishing. It's great if you can get at least two events during your day of fishing. This is what I talked about earlier about stacking up your poker chips. The more chips you can stack, the bigger the payoff. I then look at the sun and the low-light periods (sunrise and sunset). If I can get a lunar event to coincide with a sunrise or sunset, I now have an even bigger stack of chips. Stacking trigger factors is what the game is all about.

Let's look at this example of how to stack the factors. When we look at the solunar table (page 131) for the day of September 16, 2020, there are plenty of factors to consider. The first thing I see is that it's a strong lunar day. It's a day before the new moon. Right away that has my interest piqued. As we look at the factors closer, the events and how they are stacked really jump out. We have both the sun and the moon at their zeniths within thirty minutes of each other. These are very strong factors, and I would absolutely be in a spot that held fish from 11:00 a.m. to 12:30 p.m. The next thing I see that lines up are the sunset and the moonset. They fall within seven minutes of each other. This is another huge trigger factor. I'd be fishing hard in one of my known fish-holding spots between 6:00 p.m. and 7:00 p.m. If I was looking at a monthly solunar calendar at the beginning of September, this day would certainly be circled. I would really want to be out fishing with these events stacked so nicely.

This is how we start looking at factors. These are very easy to look at once you get it figured out.

We now have to look at what I call the wildcard factors. These are the factors that we have little or no control over, like the weather and other human beings. The fishing pressure factor is something we can control a little bit. One thing to keep in mind is that most educated muskie anglers also are watching the solunar tables and know when the good days are taking place. These good solunar days can have a definite effect on the amount of fishing pressure on your body of water. You might want to alter your game plan, or just know that on these high-activity days there is most likely going to be more people fishing. Remember, learn to deal with it. If you don't think this is true, I'll use the example of one of my clients who books four or five days a year with me. I'll get a text message from him, usually just before Christmas, and in it are screenshots of the solunar table he uses. In each month he has circled certain dates that he would like to book throughout the year. All of the dates are key lunar times. If he's watching them, so are a lot of other anglers, so I'll be prepared for a little more pressure on those dates.

Now that you know there is going to be fishing pressure, you can try to beat them to the punch, go to a less-pressured body if water, or just deal with it. It's not rocket science. Every angler that is going to pursue muskies knows that fishing pressure is something they'll have to manage. All bodies of water are different. It's your job to try to figure out the best way to approach pressured water. A lake angler is certainly going to approach it differently than a river angler. These are the little nuances that you'll have to learn. Just know that it's there and that you'll have to come up with some method of working this factor into your game plan.

The real wildcard will always be the weather. Because it is such a wildcard, it is really hard to try to manage your fishing around it. Things can change quickly, and they often do. Just try to do the best that you can to manage this factor—after all, it's the biggest one to consider. The only real advice that I can give is to find a weather forecasting service that you trust. Now, this is somewhat of an oxymoronic statement—after all, it is the weather—but I have one that does pretty well for me. The other thing is to find a good radar app. This might be one of the best tools a fishing guide or angler can have. I'm not a big fan of smartphones, but the radar app is one of the top reasons I still have one. It can save you from potentially dangerous situations and can tell you how close that front is and give you a good idea when those big muskies might turn on. The more you muskie fish, the more a student of the weather you will become. Look for those changes that we discussed earlier. It's all about a moving barometer and getting the timing down.

KIP VIETH

THE UNICORN DAY

What's a unicorn day? It is the mythical day that every muskie angler dreams about. Does it exist? No one knows for sure, but every now and then it seems like one is spotted. It is the day when all the trigger factors that we discussed come into play, and the seasoned muskie angler gets a strange tingling sensation. They know that something is going to happen, and come hell or high water they're going to be on the water fishing.

The day begins like any other. You know that the new moon is tomorrow, so already you are thinking about sneaking out for a little bit of fishing today. You look at the solunar tables for the day and see that everything is stacked about as good as it could be. Like the situation that we talked about earlier: moon and sun at the zenith about the same time, and a moonrise and sunset within twenty minutes of each other. Already in the back of your head you know you will most likely be out fishing for at least a few hours. Then you turn on the morning news and weather report and you see this:

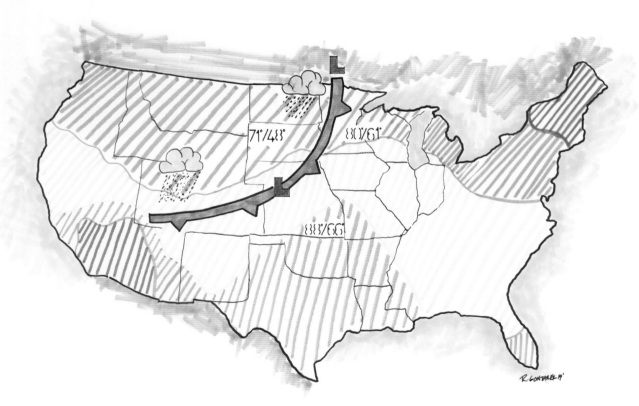

RUSS GRONTAREK

You now check the local forecast to see when that front will be moving in. It's due to arrive just after dark. It's go-time! You call into work sick, send your significant other a thoughtful gift, and call your fishing buddy and tell him to do the same. The moon and sun are almost perfect. It's a weekday, so fishing pressure will be a little less than normal, and you have a nice approaching low front with a falling barometer. We have a sighting! It might just be a unicorn day.

Now, I have had all these things lined up before and have gone out and not seen a fish. That being said, I'll take my chances on the day I just described, because when you start factoring the factors, everything points to a big trigger event. When I can stack all those factors in nice, neat columns, it's one of the best things I can do to predict a trigger event. We all know that trying to figure muskies out is a bit like chasing unicorns.

There are no rules when it comes to trying to figure out when a muskie is going to eat. They're just educated guesses. The more you pay attention to your surroundings and the factors that we just discussed, the better your guesses will become. It's still a guess, though. No one will ever figure these creatures out 100 percent. All an angler can try to do is pattern their movements, actions, seasonal activity, lunar cycles, and weather the best they can. We can just hope to get it right every once in a great while.

Kip Notes

- Put time in on the water.
- Take detailed notes of your fishing days and reference them often.
- Pay attention to your surroundings. What could affect my fishing today? Listen to your gut.
- The lunar effect is real. Learn it and how it affects your fishing.
- Factor the factors. Learn what factors affect your fisheries the most—weather is usually the key one—and stack them in your favor.

CHAPTER NINE

PUTTING IT ALL TOGETHER

PROPER RELEASE

You've read the book and practiced casting, your figure eights, and your strip-set. You have spent hours on the water and finally landed your first large muskie. Now comes perhaps the most important part of the entire game: The proper release of your trophy. The catch-and-release ethic is perhaps stronger in the muskie world than in any other circle of anglers. It is my belief that a world record may be caught but will never be killed due to this strong ethic.

We talked some about the proper tools to have in the boat in chapter 4. I try to keep those tools handy so when it does happen, they're right next to me. The net needs to be big enough to handle large fish. It is always better to go bigger than smaller. A large net lets the muskie rest easier after it has been netted. Keep the fish in the net and in the water. This allows the fish to rest a bit and calm down. I keep the fish in the water and get all my tools and camera organized so that when we go to take the hook out, everything is ready.

If possible, I try to remove the hook while the fish is in the net. With the proper tools, there is seldom a time that a muskie needs to be unhooked out of the net. Pop the hook out or cut it if you have to. This method allows the water to support the weight of the muskie. Lifting a large muskie can put more stress on the fish and its internal organs. The water keeps the muskie floating and supports it naturally. This also allows the muskie to breathe and get plenty of oxygen during this stressful period. The goal of proper release is to have the muskie out of the water as little as possible and to support the muskie properly.

After the muskie is unhooked and calmed down, it is time to lift it out of the net. A quick grab of the jawbone by the gill plate is all that's needed. When you have a

This is all you're left with if you don't hold your muskie properly: a body full of muskie slime and a frown.
MARK OLSON

firm grip (here's where the fish-handling gloves come in handy), simply lift the musk-ie's head out and slide your other hand under the fish's belly. Snap the grip-and-grin photo and quickly and gently get the muskie back into the water.

Depending on how stressed the fish is, you may have to revive it a bit. During the summer months when the water is warmer, this may take some time. Try to get the muskie in calmer water. The stress of the wave action and current can sometimes make it difficult to revive a muskie. This is one time that I will sometimes use a BogaGrip. It is really the only time that I use it other than building leaders. It's a nice tool for reviving fish. You can maintain good control of the fish and not put a lot of strain on them. When they are ready to go, just unclip them and let them slide back to their homes.

Just like everything in this game, practice makes perfect, and with this practice everyone is happy—after all, you just landed a muskie. Seeing that big of a fish in a landing net can be pretty daunting. Just relax and stay calm (I know that's a lot to ask) and think of the fish. Keep that muskie in the water as much as possible and as calm as possible. The more you fish, the more fish you'll come in contact with. The future of the fishery and sport are incumbent on how you handle those fish. Do the best possible job you can to make sure that the fish you just caught can be caught again. Also, remember that fishing is a blood sport, believe it or not. Stuff happens, and sooner or later one will not make it. Just learn from it and hopefully it will never happen again. Sharp objects in fish's mouths will eventually kill one. It's tough, but it happens. Just do your best and 99 percent of the time the fish will swim away to live and fight another day.

UNDERSTANDING YOURSELF AS AN ANGLER

I think one of the most important things in fly fishing for muskies is to set goals. These can be very fluid, and as you grow as a muskie angler, they will most likely change. Understanding your goals will help you understand yourself as an angler. It's a barometer of where you're at when it comes to fishing. Also know that there is no shame in any goal that you set for yourself. They are your goals, and that's all that matters.

When I first started muskie fishing, I was probably a little different from most beginners. I wanted to catch a muskie over 45 inches. I set my goals extremely high and it was very humbling, which is good. My first muskie was 36 inches, and I was a little let down by the experience. I guess I'd seen a lot of smaller fish, and I just didn't really have that much interest in them. "Go big or go home" has been my motto for most of my fishing career. I certainly took a bigger bite of the apple than I should have when I first got serious about muskies. It hasn't always been that way. I can still

Looks like Mark learned the hard way.
MARK OLSON

remember the 10-inch brook trout that was the first fish I caught on a fly I tied. I can take you to the exact spot if you asked me to. I am just as proud of that fish as I am of the biggest muskie that I've ever caught. Goals change, and that is all good. What I'm trying to say is you should set a goal and do the work to accomplish it.

If your goal is to simply catch a muskie on the fly, God bless you. If your goal is to catch a 45-plus–inch muskie, God bless you. No goal is any better than the other. It's your goal and that's all that matters. Your goal should set up your fishing. If your goal is to get a muskie on the fly, then I would probably send you to certain waters; if it is to get a big fish, I would send you elsewhere. Your goals should dictate your fishing and how you approach it. By studying and knowing what your goals are, you can best accomplish them. Just be honest with yourself and realize there are no bad goals when it comes to fishing. You're not competing against anyone. I saw a great quote the other day that said that the only fly angler that you should be competing with is the one you were yesterday. The thing is to just keep getting better. As you get better and more skilled, your goals will evolve and grow. The journey and growth are what makes muskie fly fishing, or any fishing for that matter, fun. Set your goals and attack them the best way you can.

We all have biases, strengths, and weaknesses. Understanding these will go a long way in helping you become a successful muskie fly angler. My bias is for rivers. I love them and the moving water. A lot of fly anglers feel this way just because we started fly fishing on rivers. Now, I will fish lakes and calm water, but it's not as fun for me as floating down a river in my drift boat. That is where I'm most comfortable. My other bias is that I don't consider it a muskie unless it's over 40 inches long. That's my bias and it has nothing to do with anything else. It's kind of like a permit. I've never caught one and have only chased them once. If I caught a small one, I would probably say that I caught one, but I wouldn't be terribly thrilled about it. That is me and no one else. Now, if one of my guides was fishing with me and caught a small muskie, I'd let them know, but that's just good old-fashioned ribbing among friends. There is no right or wrong—it is just what you like. Be honest with yourself and know that we all have biases. Some of us (me) are just a little more vocal than others about them.

Bias can be weaknesses, and my reluctance to fish a lake is one bias that I work to get over. There are a lot of big fish in lakes, and I mean a lot. Probably more than in

Time with friends and drift boats is hard to beat.
MIKE DVORAK

a river, to be perfectly honest with you. My being just a little uncomfortable fishing nonmoving water is something that I have been trying to get over. That bias has cost me a lot of good fishing opportunities just because I'm out of my comfort zone. It's something that I struggle with and have been trying to work on. I know that this is a weakness, and if you understand your weaknesses, you can attack them as well. Yours might be casting or strip-setting. It doesn't really matter, just as long as you accept them and work on them. Remember what I've said about practice. We like to fish the way we like to fish. Being uncomfortable is hard, but it is how we get better.

You have to be comfortable in your style and philosophies of fishing or you just won't have a good time doing it. Remember, this is supposed to be fun, and if it isn't you won't be doing it for long. That being said, you also have to challenge yourself to get uncomfortable. Maybe take an hour out of your day to work on something that doesn't come easy to you. Go practice casting an hour a week. Instead of fishing your same water, go to a different fishery every fifth time you go out. It doesn't have to be that hard. It's work and it's uncomfortable, but it will make you a better angler. You have to be disciplined, however, to make it happen. If you're not a disciplined angler, a muskie will find a way to exploit that sooner or later. Have fun and make sure that you are always learning. One good thing about muskie fly fishing is that there is always something to learn.

Make a list of things that you need to work on, and it will go a long way in improving your fishing. The front of your journal is a great place to keep it. Here is my list of things that I need to work on. The first one should tell you a lot.

1. Keeping a better journal
2. Fishing still water
3. Concentration
4. Keeping better relationships with other guides and friends. It's important to learn from others no matter how long you have been doing this.

It's pretty simple, but it is a nice reminder of things that you might need to address throughout the season. It will keep you grounded and make it easier to understand yourself as an angler.

UNDERSTANDING THE FISH

This might be more important than any other thing that you can do in muskie fishing. Muskies aren't that hard to pattern if you know where to look and what to look for. They're predictable creatures for the most part. If you know where the fish are, half the battle is over. Now comes the hard part: getting one of them to eat.

My friend Troy, who got me started in muskie on the fly, had two sayings. When I was first fishing with him, the sayings would drive me nuts. I just thought they were more guide BS than anything else, but the longer I do this, the more sense they make. They are "Never leave fish to find fish" and "It only takes one." When you're first learning the game, you just want a fish to eat your fly and you really don't care about cute little sayings. But the more you do it, the more they make sense. If you have the fish patterned and know where they are hunting, don't go looking for more. After all, it only takes one fish to make your day, let alone an entire season.

We sometimes have a tendency to overthink it. Trust your gut, and back your gut up with science and logic. We talked about the basics of the muskie's biology throughout the book, and it will point you in the right direction. Become a student of the fish. It will go a long way toward making you a successful muskie angler. Look for the four basic needs of a muskie that we talked about, and you'll find them. Again, they are:

1. Making more muskies
2. Finding food sources
3. Staying comfortable
4. Not working too hard

A few words about fishing pressure. Of all the factors that we have discussed, this might be the biggest hurdle to jump in the future. I know we talked about it earlier in the book. We said that muskies have no natural predators and that is true, but we forgot about us. Yes, we are predators. Muskies probably more than any other fish will adjust their behaviors, feeding times, and even where they call home if they are feeling pressured. Remember, flies have an advantage on some waters simply because the muskies haven't seen a lot of them and they are something very different. But also remember that on some waters fly fishing is the main way that muskies are pursued. These fish have seen a lot of feathers and flash. Try to keep it fresh no matter where you are fishing. Think a bit outside the box. On a very pressured body of water, it might be a different fly or lure that triggers them to eat. There is no silver bullet, just hard work and looking for a different fly or spot that is far from the madding crowd.

TIME ON THE WATER

The "Understanding the Fish" section was pretty short. That is because if you know just the basics, time on the water will teach you the rest. If you take anything away from this book, know this: Nothing beats quality time on the water. It is the single most important thing in any type of fishing that you choose to pursue. If you never read this book, watched a video, listened to a presentation, or had a friend help you, it really wouldn't matter. Spending time on the water will eventually teach you every- thing you really need to know to be successful. It would most likely be a very painful process, but you'd get there. All this book or any other form of education is doing is simply trying to shrink the learning curve and put you on the right path to success.

Anyone can debate the best ways to teach or if the things that we try to teach are really useful. There might be things in this book that you think aren't practical for you, and that is probably going to be true in some cases. The only way that you're

SOMETIMES IT'S AFTER YOUR TIME
ON THE WATER THAT SOME OF THE
BEST MEMORIES ARE MADE.
JON LUKE

going to figure that out is by putting your time in on the water and paying those all-too-painful dues. We've all had to do it, some more than others. If you're serious about being successful, get serious about spending as much time as possible on the water.

I know that everyone is in different places in their lives. Kids, parents, work, school, significant other—they all have to be dealt with, and it can be difficult to juggle all of them along with a muskie addiction. Just know that if you get a pass to fish, use it. If you are limited to a set amount of time due to life, use it wisely. Fish smart. Make the best use of the time you have on the water. Come up with a game plan, work on a different tactic, find new water—it's all good, just be smart about it. Time with your new best friend or evil addiction, depending on how you look at it, will help you learn more and become a better angler.

CONSERVATION AND ETHICS

It saddens me that I even have to put this in this book. I'm going to start out by saying that despite what you think, no one owns the waters or the fish that swim in them. They are open to everyone, and we should all remember that when we run into someone who is also enjoying a day on the water. This shouldn't be a problem anywhere, but every once in a while it rears its ugly head. If everyone would just respect the space of everyone else, things would be a lot simpler.

Muskie on the fly is a rapidly growing part of fly fishing, and things aren't going to be like they were five years ago. I have to be honest, it even frustrates me at times. We all have to just realize that a muskie can never have too many friends. We love them, and we should give as much respect to our fellow anglers as we do the fish. If you think you might be upsetting someone by your actions, you probably are. It's nothing a little communication wouldn't cure. It's really not that hard. Respect the people that paved the way for you. We all had someone at one point or another that took us under their wing and showed us the ropes, so to speak. It's not about an Instagram post or trying to impress someone. I hate to break it to you, but as my buddy Russ says, no one is that special. Play nice, treat others like you want to be treated, and remember it's only a fish.

It might only be a fish, but it's a pretty special one. As I mentioned earlier, the catch-and-release ethic is alive and very much well in the muskie world. State game and fish departments are even realizing this and are implementing some very impressive regulations to ensure that there will be muskies for many generations that follow. I'm proud of my home state of Minnesota for leading the charge and having some of the best regulations in the country for muskies. A big muskie is a rare animal and should be treated as such. Handle them with care. Remember that muskie fishing is always about the muskie. If we keep that in mind, it will do them a great deal of good. If you are so inclined and would like to help with their conservation, the group Muskies Inc. is doing most of the heavy lifting when it comes to conservation of the species and the many issues muskies face. I would encourage you to join them in their fight for this magnificent fish. They have done a ton of research, some of it used in this book, to try to help both anglers and muskies.

Research is also being carried out by a number of states and Canadian provinces. Muskies are a very mysterious fish, and there is still much to learn about them and their habits and habitats. Fisheries biologists do wonderful work, and I encourage every muskie angler to reach out to them. As I have stated, they have a wealth of knowledge and can help every muskie angler no matter how experienced they are. It would also be nice to thank them for all their hard work. They are underappreciated by most anglers.

A muskie is just too rare to not share with others. Take good care of the resource, and we will all be better for it.

Kip Notes

- Put time in on the water.
- Practice catch-and-release. Large muskies are rare and should be handled with care. Learn how to properly handle them.
- Learn about yourself as an angler and what you need to work on. Face your weaknesses and turn them into strengths.
- Respect other anglers and the ones that paved the way for all of us. It's not about your Instagram account or your clients—it's simply about the magnificent fish. Remember, no one is that special.
- Support muskie conservation efforts.

CHAPTER TEN

A DIFFERENT VIEW

Muskie anglers are as different as the waters they fish throughout North America. I fish a very small part of the muskie world in the grand scheme of things. I thought that it would be a great idea to hear from other anglers about their thoughts and the waters that they fish. Some of the authors are friends of mine, and others I've never had the pleasure of meeting in person. I did know that I wanted to get their insights on muskie fishing, though. It's always good to get another point of view. You always can learn something from others.

FIRST TIME OUT

Bob White

That summer in southwest Alaska, where I guide, was miserable. It had rained for ninety continuous days. On more than one morning I awoke in the dark to the sound of rain pounding on the roof of my small and dank cabin. Nothing in it ever dried completely, and I'd learned to hang my long johns and fleece top upside down the night before to allow the previous day's soaking to collect in the cuffs and sleeves. These were wrung out in a coffee can next to my bed. I shivered at the thought of pulling on the damp clothes.

When I walked down to the shack next to the dock, where the crew gathered to collect their thoughts for the day, one of my brother-guides was standing directly in the downpour off the tin roof, drinking a cold (and now highly diluted) cup of coffee.

"What the hell are you doing?" I asked. "Get under the roof where it's dry!"

"What the f— for?" he replied. "I woke up wet and cold, and I'll be that way all day, and tomorrow, and the day after . . . until I finally get home."

Upon my return home in the fall, I was ready to be warm and dry, and not guide for a very long while . . . like for nine months.

When I noticed that the closing words of an email message from my friend Kip Vieth said that he was "looking forward to guiding with you next week," I asked my wife, Lisa, "Do you know anything about a guide-trip next weekend?"

There was more than a bit of panic in my voice.

"Sure," she replied. "Don't you remember telling Kip, before you left for Alaska this spring, that you were going to help him with a big group of musky fishermen?"

"I told him I'd *think* about it," I said. "I haven't guided for muskies all that much, and I don't want to come off like a jerk."

When I realized that I was trapped, I shook my lowered head. "What's the weather supposed to be like?" I asked, finally accepting the inevitable, but hoping to at least stay dry.

"It's supposed to be cold and rainy, with high winds," Lisa replied. "Do you want me to bake some cookies for your shore lunches?"

"Sure." It was all I could think to say.

I arrived at camp late (I'd gotten lost along the way), met my fishermen for the following day, and had a few beers as I caught up with some old friends. Eventually, they showed me a map of the river I'd never floated and explained how the shuttle would work.

I became disoriented the next morning while driving to the river; I couldn't recall how many times I'd crossed it. Upon our arrival at the landing we loaded up, and I began to mistakenly push the boat upstream. It was a bit of a struggle, of course, but I told myself that the wind was stronger than it looked. After a hundred yards or so, one of the young fishermen (they were brothers) politely asked why we were going upstream, when it was his understanding that I'd left the truck and trailer downstream.

"It's the wind," I replied with false bravado. "It's blowing much stronger than it looks." Then, as I watched a maple leaf float past underwater, I realized that I was an asshole who didn't know upstream from down.

It must have shown on my face because the other brother asked, "You've done this before, right? I mean, guided for musky?"

It was time to come clean. "Nope . . . not really."

"But you've guided . . . right?"

"A little bit," I replied. "Look, let's just all do our best and make a day out of it."

We had a nice float and actually moved one fish, which didn't eat.

That evening, it was announced over dinner that the following day I'd fish with Bill, the father of the disenchanted brothers whom I'd just guided. I think dad had decided to fall on the sword for the sake of his boys. Still, he was a good enough guy . . . and we hit it off just fine. His buddy, Jim, seemed decent enough too.

Since I'd been on the river for one whole day and had its direction down pat, I went to bed feeling good about what might come.

In the morning, we moved four really good musky within 200 yards of the landing, but had no eats. Then it happened; a good fish blew up on Bill's fly and we had a musky hooked for a few seconds . . . before it came unbuttoned.

Just minutes later Jim tossed his fly into a tangled deadfall. As he stripped it clear a 40-plus-inch musky exploded on it, and the water erupted. Jim's rod bent double as the line came tight . . . and then went sickeningly slack. The toothy bastard had cut through my 80-pound shock tippet like a hot knife through butter.

Shit.

We rowed back up to the top of the pool for a second drift, but before we could cast, the big fish free-jumped 20 feet from us, shaking his head in a frantic effort to rid himself of the fly we'd left in his mouth.

That's musky for "Screw you!"

Two casts later, while doing a deep figure eight under the boat, Bill announced that he was stuck fast to the bottom. But the bottom suddenly moved upstream.

We were solidly hooked to a good fish, and the fish went deep . . . where it stayed for a long time before Bill worked him to the surface and we got a look.

My new best friend played the big fish well, and before you knew it, there was a musky on the beach.

Without a tape, we reckoned the fish to be about 50 inches. Not a bad start; my buddy's first musky . . . and mine too! Both of our hands were shaking so badly that when we went for a high-five, we nearly missed each other and fell down in a heap. Jim snapped off a few photographs before we released it, and we marked an oar with the fish's length . . . to be taped later. It turned out to be less than we thought, but just barely.

There's an old adage that goes, "You know it's a really good fish when your guide wants to have his photo taken with it" . . . and I shamelessly did.

We decide to repeat the drift one last time, and as I pushed upstream, Bill continued to cast. As his fly drew near the boat, my oar came down on another musky, hitting him squarely between the eyes. I got soaked from an eruption of water, and the fish was gone.

The clouds melted away with the passing hours, and as the sky turned blue the bite turned off.

It was a nice enough float. Bill sat quietly in the back of the boat and basked in the glow of his great fish, leaving most of the water to his buddy. Except for the odd smallmouth bass, things were pretty quiet. We didn't tag many bass, but those we did were all big and in great shape.

At the last bend before our landing, Bill announced that perhaps he'd make one or two more casts. As the low sun warmed the sandbank to our front, he limbered up his rod and made the cast. The fly danced seductively toward the boat . . . where it disappeared in an enormous boil.

One last cast . . . one last musky!

Not bad for my first time out!

VISES AND VICES

Russ Grontarek

Definition of vise:
1: any of various tools with two jaws for holding work that close usually by a screw, lever, or cam

Definition of vice:
1a: moral depravity or corruption: wickedness; b: a moral fault or failing; c: a habitual and usually trivial defect

Homophones are a type of homonym that sound alike and have different meanings, but also have different spellings.

I start with a few facts of the English language, as it sets a weight at the other end of the measure. From here I focus on a touch and feel equation that comes from an intimate perspective.

Recently my wife and I had our first child. We do what we can to rear him true and escape the selfish side of our nature. We hope for the best. Peering inward to habits (hobbies), passions, addictions, percolate a few confusions about how he will view us and more precisely me. My wife is close to sainthood, so say my buddies, and that's all the further I'll go.

Last year, I spent over forty days on the water with a borrowed wood drift boat, hunting river muskies in Minnesota and Wisconsin. I have a full-time job and do not guide for money. It takes a certain mindset and (ill) character to put yourself through this. If you've ever found yourself fortunate enough to chase freshwater's apex fish out of a drift boat, you may just forget about your history as a "fisher person." To luck and gift, my comrades and I were able to boat twenty-eight fish with half of those being over 42 inches. This creates a hard to get rid of infection, even when your child is about to be born.

A week before my son was born, I was on a drift when I was fortunate enough to catch my largest fish of the season. To see these archaic dinosaurs of freshwater is in one word "healing." These fish always surprise me with their size and speed of attack. A lot has been written and spoken of late about why these fish are seeing more flies these days. I will only paint a quick picture. A 267 cast, an 11-weight, a 13-inch double, strip, strip, strip, strip, set . . . chaos! As an aside, I am not a fish-or-die, chainsaw personality. I will not leave my wife or child on the side of the road due to this form of entertainment or for that matter, ditch my responsibilities at work. It just means that when I have free time, you know where I will be. Oh, and the definition of free time might flex a little from time to time. Sorry brothers, there are enough kids out there without fathers.

This passion means hours at the vise concocting and scheming different ideas of success. As the moons aligned, so did my friendship with the best fly tier and muskie junkie I have run across. If the people who know you best list the top three things you are thankful for at Thanksgiving as muskie, whiskey, and we'll leave the last one out for etiquette's sake, you possibly have a problem; he does. No judging on my behalf, as I aspire to create the art he does at the vise and on the water.

This is where the two words and definitions collide, and the true essence of this literary hogwash begins. When constructing the true 15-inch double leviathans we commit to, there is time. Where there is time, there is thought. Empty thought sometimes tricks the mind into believing it needs to be filled. Filled with the kind of vices I have so long committed to as a 35-year-old human with insecurities, stress, wanting, and general wearing down from the lathe of life. I like my vices of high ABV beer, whiskey, and cigarettes. We share these vices with all things muskie, and it creates a commonality and normality with us. As the night grows long, the subjects change from light to dark and this representation shows in our doubles. I know I am talking to people who are nodding their cartoon bubble heads and have been here before, and long to get there again soon. Now is the finicky part, though. By using certain terminology we avoid medical and treatable forms of the scary word "addiction." We avoid these terms, but I will let you know that there are things I am unwilling to do without. Addiction and passion intermingle with one another, each with their own unique reputation. One being the trashy leather miniskirt and the other the classy black dress hiding the freak inside. We only judge one because we fear her. The other gets a pass and we cover for her because we might be able to show her to the ones we love. It's a fine line we walk, my friends, in the 256 shades of gray.

If you fish enough, you understand there is no better teacher than the elusive time on the water. But the time on the water pales in comparison to the time and work it takes to be productive when you get there. Enjoyment takes its form in the prep, tying, strategy, weather watching, lunar gazing, map reading, and smack talking with your fellow brethren. Talk about vices. The layers in which this excuse to connect with the outdoors and like-minded fellows are not astronomical. We haven't even talked about boats yet. Jon boat, drift boat, canoe, skiff, skanoe, kayak, SUP board, low side, high side, prop, jet oars, cooler, anchors, trailer. I'm not even going to touch rods, reels, and lines. In the aioli of my fishing are all of these in a cog and sprocket idea of what is right. Few people fit into it, so I hope that my son will someday understand this enjoyment, and we will share in it together. I know some people would call these demons. Fair enough. I call them friends.

Writing this has been self-indulgent and cathartic. I guess the question is, what is in your vise, and what vice is you in? Abraham Lincoln once said, "It has been my experience that folks who have no vices have very few virtues."

Addendum written in 2019

Six years have passed, and I am still scheming, dreaming, and toiling after my sharp-toothed friends. Things have changed a bit. My wife (now a confirmed saint) and I have two boys I lovingly call the "east side riff-raff." My hope is that, at the very least, one of them finds this sport interesting enough to share some evenings on a boat with me water hauling and laughing.

Some things never seem to change. I have held firm to some vices, while relieving some others of their duties. One tends to find out, maybe with age or error, that these friends tend to cause harm to the ones around you and yourself. Can't change the past, no riddle there, but now the present seems to be better while sipping back in moderation. There's a well-known quote: "You can't soar with the eagles in the morning if you're out at night with the turkeys." Luckily, I have found some eagles who act like turkeys now and again, and that suits me just fine.

When the times are tough, fish. When the times are good, fish. I'm sure you will find looking back, that those times will not be a waste. Expect the fish and waters to understand what you're going through. After all, our ancestors mutated and decided land was a good place to be. It doesn't mean that we don't feel the calling to turn back and forget our thumbs for a while.

The rhythm of life sometimes makes me feel as though I am not in step. I would rather be off-key on the water.

VIRGINIA WATERS

Matt Miles

We are blessed here in Virginia to have so many types of fisheries and species. Around ten years ago muskie fishing on the fly became very popular. With the new popularity came more anglers and new muskie anglers to Virginia waters. Virginia has three popular muskie rivers: the New, James, and Shenandoah. There are also some small lakes in Virginia where muskies were stocked. Over the years I have seen more and more muskies in smaller tributaries where they were not stocked. Their need to seek out colder water has led them into smaller rivers and creeks for the summer months and some stay year-round.

Our summers are very warm and humid here in the Southeast. When water temps get above 75 degrees, muskies tend to find the colder springs and creeks to lay in for the extra oxygen. I generally will not fish or guide for muskies after the month of May. When the water temps are above 75 degrees, the fish have a higher risk of not reviving after the fight. When you care about a fish or fishery, you need to just lay off it or find another species to target that the warm water doesn't bother. I consider "Muskie Season" October through the second week of March. Our fall and winter provide the best fishing during the year. I especially like mid-November. Once water temps get down to 50 degrees, our muskies have moved into their wintering holes. Now you have a lot more muskies in one area, which brings your chances up to catch one. I've seen firsthand, while shocking muskies with the Department of Game and Inland Fisheries, the quantity of muskies in a large wintering hole. My first time doing it we shocked twenty-eight muskies out of one area. Most years the muskie spawn will begin mid-March or once water temps sustain around 50 degrees. Once the spawn begins, I leave them alone to do their thing.

The James River is the one I call home. The James was stocked in 1972 with muskies and continued stocking until 2009. Biologists began to find the muskies reproducing successfully on their own and the population had good numbers. I would say the majority of muskies caught now on the James River are wild fish. On the James you will find good numbers of fish in the 35- to 42-inch size range, but there are plenty of fish past 42 inches into that fish-of-a-lifetime size, 50 inches. I prefer muskie fishing the James because of its size and depth. The river is not extremely deep or wide, so for the fly angler it makes covering the water easier.

Virginia muskies prefer the same things as the muskies do in other states. Structure like eddies, ledges, grass, points, and down trees are worth the cast. In early fall you will still have muskies just about anywhere—shallow, deep, and riffles—so just fish it all during that time frame. When the water temps drop to 50 degrees, that's when I focus on deep wintering holes. I'll fish a hole from the start to the tail out, both banks, and the middle of the river. You have to cover the water to find that hungry fish. The more water you can cover with the boat and with your cast, the better.

Sometimes people refer to permit fishing as being similar to muskie. The fact is, it's hard to get them both to eat your fly, but you don't make the cast until you see the permit, and with muskies you must cast to see them. Both fish are tough mentally, but muskie fishing is also tough on the body making long casts all day. Doing the figure eight is a must with this fishery. I teach my anglers to do it every cast regardless of what they see or don't see on the retrieve. Year after year 30 percent of the muskies landed in my boat the fish ate on the figure eight. Like most diehard muskie fishermen, I have seen fish come out of nowhere to eat the fly. Sometimes you may be floating over a muskie during your figure eight and that brings the fish up. Yes, it gets old, but just do it and you will be rewarded at some point. Because believe me, the time you get lazy and you don't figure eight is when the big fish will show, and you'll miss your chance.

I have had many clients catch their first muskie the first time they tried. I have had others go a few trips before it happens. Usually you will have some muskies follow the fly back to the boat during the day. Follows vary; I have seen over twenty different follows in a day, and I've seen just one follow all day. I'd say on average you'll see three to ten different muskies follow on most days in Virginia.

The follow has always made me wonder. Fish have to get more energy from their food than they use to get it. So why does a muskie follow a fly without eating? I think sometimes its curiosity, territorial, and of course hunger. Usually you can tell the serious fish following from the not so serious. It's typically the speed they're coming in. If the fish is moving fast to catch up to the fly, there's a good chance it's going to eat. Slow, hanging way back or deep under the fly follows typically mean just a sighting for me, but I treat them all the same and try to get a reaction on the figure eight. I once did the figure eight around ten times and the fish just kept spinning around with it. I was getting tired and thinking what next, so I just did a circle with the fly and the fish ate it. If the muskie is there, don't give up. My rule is if the fish goes under the boat, keep doing the figure eight. I've seen them pop right back out and eat. Another key to success with the figure eight is to have your fly the same depth as the fish when you figure eight. Make it easy on the fish because they will not make it easy on you.

I really believe that muskie fly fishing is nothing more than being in the right place at the right time. As a guide I can get you in the right place—it's the timing that's the hard part. Muskies can go three to five days without feeding, so it's literally about being there when the fish are hungry. I have favorite flies or colors that give me confidence, but I also believe they'll eat anything when the mood strikes. It really boils down to putting your time in with these fish. As fly fishermen we choose to do it the hard way, so remember that it's not going to be easy. You have to enter the trip or day with confidence, aggressiveness, and realistic expectations. With muskie you have to roll with the punches and not take it too seriously or you will burn out. Know it's hard and give it all you've got, and the fish will come to the net.

BREAKING DOWN BIG WATER FOR MUSKIE

Eric Grajewski

Captain Eric Grajewski spent much of his youth spin fishing on Lake St. Clair (LSC) and rivers throughout the upper and lower peninsulas of Michigan. As he got older his passion for fly fishing grew, and streamer fishing was a huge part of that. After graduating from college, he moved back to the lake he grew up loving. Combining his love for fly fishing and Lake St. Clair, it seemed like the perfect fit and it WAS! Having spent many years fishing LSC, he has a vast knowledge of the lake and the experience to chase species such as muskie, pike, smallmouth and largemouth bass, white bass, and sturgeon. But what he specializes in and loves to do is chase muskie with a fly rod!

Locating structure that is not obvious can pay off, as it did in this case with this fish coming off of a nice rock pile.
ERIC GRAJEWSKI

The first thing I do when I approach a large body of water is search for structure. This is probably the most obvious to fishermen. You find structure, you find fish. There is your visual structure, which can be rocky or sandy shorelines, weeds or a log sticking out of the water, and shoreline points. These spots are easy to find and are worth fishing, but they can get fished a lot because they are so obvious. The other type of structure is the structure that you can't always see with the naked eye. This is where electronics are so important. Use your electronics for locating a patch of weeds or a rock pile in deeper water. Structure can be as small as a slight change in the bottom, such as changing from sand to rock or even just a 6-inch change in the depth of the water. Much like reading a river's water current where you have seams and

A large fish that came from some isolated weeds and forage out in the middle of the lake

ERIC GRAJEWSKI

pockets, think of the bottom of the lake in the same way. Much of the time this type of structure that can't be seen is the water that will hold larger fish.

Just as important as finding structure in a large lake is finding forage (bait). Forage can be shad, suckers, minnows, or panfish. Muskies are predators. They will be in areas where there are good amounts of forage. Some lakes have many structure locations and some have very little to none. Having great structure with lots of bait is ideal, but you aren't going to always have that. Use your electronics or even visually look for bait. This sometimes can be out in the middle of the lake with no structure, but there is lots of bait. Don't be afraid to try those spots even when they seem like they are in the middle of nowhere. You will be surprised how often these spots hold fish, and many times lots of fish.

Two characteristics of flies that are important to me are movement and color. If I had to pick one that is probably more important, I would say most of the time it is fly movement over color. I typically like a fly that glides back and forth with each strip. That's not to say a fly that rides straight or dives up or down won't have its day, I just have found that flies that have this glide movement seem to get the most action from fish. When it comes to color choice, I try to have one angler fish something dark (usually solid black, black and red, or black and orange) and something light or natural (yellows, whites, tans). If I am going to change color, it is usually going to be a drastic change like going from dark to light or light to dark. Going with a couple colors you have confidence in and that have worked for you in the past is usually better than changing a bunch of times. Much of the time it isn't going to be the color you have on that isn't working, but more that the fish aren't active at that time.

This fish couldn't resist a black with orange and red fly.

ERIC GRAJEWSKI

Most of the time anglers are going to use the conventional strip/pause retrieve. This works much of the time, but don't be afraid to mix in a two-handed retrieve. This is tucking the rod under your arm and with both hands stripping in the line hand over hand. It doesn't always have to be a fast burn, as sometimes they just want a steady fleeing baitfish versus imitating a wounded/dying baitfish. There are days where this is the only retrieve that will get a fish to eat. This is a retrieve that can be successful on rivers too, especially ones with slower current.

I am a big believer in the idea that muskies generally have feeding "windows" most days. Once in a while, you get the great day where fish are active all day. But most of the time you will find that they are really only active during smaller parts of the day. These windows may last an hour or two or can be as short as twenty minutes. These can be brought on by a weather change or moon phase, but many times it is not totally understood why this happens. So keep in mind that just because you didn't move any fish when you fished a specific area in the lake does not mean the fish weren't there. They may not have been active at that particular time of the day. If you have an area that has really good structure or lots of bait and you didn't see any fish, revisit that spot multiple times throughout the day. Sooner or later you will hit that spot at the correct time when the fish are active.

Unlike some fish, muskies will not always follow or eat every time a fly or bait crosses their face, even when presented perfectly. I mostly fish a lake that at any given time I know there can be fifty-plus fish in that area, and I will fish sunup to sundown and may only get two twenty-minute windows throughout the whole day where those fish decide to start moving. So keep hitting those higher confidence spots. Sooner or later they will pay off. The great thing about fly fishing for muskie is that catching one fish on a fly can make a day. So keep at it no matter how slow

On this day the anglers went hours without seeing anything, and then within forty-five minutes landed three fish.

ERIC GRAJEWSKI

the day is going. It only takes one cast to make a day that seems like it is sucking a day you won't forget!

NOTES FROM THE OLD MASTER

Bill Sherer

I'm now in my fourth decade of chasing muskies with the fly rod, and I have no intentions of turning back. When I first began in the 1970s, there was very little information concerning the sport, and most definitely no one I could look to for inspiration or direction. I did the next best thing and gathered my intel from anywhere I could. The field was limited, but musky fishing with gear has a rich history, so I began there.

Growing up during my high school years in Boulder Junction, Wisconsin, gave me access to some of the very best well-known guides from the era of the "Old Time Musky Wranglers." Those storied guides who really lived the lore and allure of musky fishing were very willing to share some of their knowledge; perhaps those old masters could see something new on the horizon.

Gleaning as much practical information and inside tactics as I could, I set out to pursue those beasts in my style with a fly rod. In short order, I learned I could not imitate the same actions of a bucktail or a Suick with a fly. I also quickly figured out that my 8-weight fly rod was woefully inadequate. It took me another five or six years to come to grips with the limitations of the equipment and to develop flies as well as a style that served my desire to attract muskies with my own patterns on a consistent basis.

Since those early days, I have found many ways to achieve my goals and to share the knowledge that I have gleaned from all my experiences. It has been a great ride that still continues.

Sometime around the late 1990s, the word finally got out from me and others with similar desires that there was an exciting sport to be had chasing these magnificent fish on the fly. That seemed to garner the attention of fly anglers from across the globe, and the floodgates were opened to everyone.

New lines, more-useful rods, better leaders, and more education on casting has advanced this sport faster than many ever imagined. An explosion of new ideas— some good, some less so—were presented to be sifted through. The good ideas made it to the top; the others were discarded. Some of those discarded ideas were put on the shelf, waiting for the time when more innovations in gear would make them viable. It seems this sport is always in motion, and innovation is necessary as the fish get more accustomed to seeing our flies and presentations.

In recent years, I have seen yet another change in which improvements in tackle have pushed the size of flies, and tactics are once again following more closely those of the gear guys. As an "old-schooler," I believe this recent fad will again drift back toward our roots, and the real essence of fly fishing will come back into vogue. I love innovation and have made my reputation on it, but in my opinion, "run and gun" is not as productive as intelligently covering the water. We'll always have innovators. We need them, and I don't mean that we should ever remain stagnant in our desire to become more efficient. Let's just not forget our roots in the process of advancement.

We all still have a very long way to go, and gathering more information from every source available is imperative for anyone hoping to land perhaps the most temperamental and challenging predator fish in North America.

TENNESSEE TITANS

An Interview with James Johnsey

Kip Vieth: Tell me about the waters that you fish in Tennessee and throughout the southern region of the United States.

James Johnsey: We are really blessed here in the South. We have so many really spectacular fisheries. They range from stream trout to bass, stripers, and muskies. Probably a lot like the waters in the Upper Midwest, we have a wide variety of waters. From small creeks to large rivers, lakes, and reservoirs, we have waters that can satisfy every angler's desires with many quality fish throughout.

KV: Tell me about the smaller creeks and rivers. They hold a special place for me. I love hunting muskies in these special places.

JJ: The cool thing about smaller creeks is that they're fun to explore and the shallow water holds some exciting fishing. We run the smaller creeks with floating lines that allow us to fish in and around wood, shallow riffles, boulder fields, etc. Think of small-mouth fishing, only for muskie. It's a whole lot of fun.

KV: How do you approach the beginning of your day?

JJ: Because the biomass of our waters changes on a monthly, weekly, and even daily basis, we approach every day by fishing all topography of the river for the first half of the day. We try soft water, soft insides, deep holes, fast riffles, cliff walls, and wood, and we don't pass up any opportunity to try to unlock the biomass that the river is holding that particular day. This maximizes our potential opportunities to find muskie. For the remainder of the day we can concentrate on the one certain pattern of topography that is holding our fish. This topography should work well for several days in a row.

KV: Sounds like muskies are pretty much the same down there. Find the bait and you'll find the fish. Getting them to eat is another thing. What are some keys to finding fish? I mean, the summer heat must make it pretty hard at times.

JJ: Tennessee is one of the most southern locations in the country where muskies reside, and being a southern region, for a coldwater species we really have to do our homework in finding springs and creek mouths that provide cooler temperatures. That research can be crucial to success in finding our target.

KV: When the water temperature rises here in the Midwest during the heat of the summer, we back off a bit. I would imagine that is the case for you guys too.

JJ: Being a southern region for this native fish, we do take extreme care in protecting the species. Some of our cooler rivers and reservoirs enable year-round fishing, but not all of our reservoirs or watersheds that hold a good population of muskies stay cool for each season. Once our river temperatures get up to the mid-70s and above, we have a high mortality rate for muskies. We keep current on our water temperatures in this region before chasing the fish on certain watersheds. Our prime season is during the winter months, both for a great bite and for the preservation of the species.

KV: I've seen some of the flies that you guys use down in the southern region and they are a lot different from the beasts that we throw up here in the Upper Midwest. Can you explain that to me?

JJ: During our muskie season, we don't have much algae plume in the water. We also don't have much of the tannic water that a lot of the country has where muskies reside. Our waters can be crystal clear in the winter during prime season, depending on rain and other factors. Something that allows us to be extremely successful is the size of our flies. We spend ample amounts of time studying the prey in our rivers. On our clear winter water days, we downsize our flies to actual bait-size fish that muskies will be eating on a regular basis. These clear waters can provide constant opportunities on 4- to 6-inch flies that live in our watersheds, from panfish and darters to gizzard shads and creek chubs. Don't be afraid to tie on a crawfish pattern or a 4-inch sculpin pattern. When waters are running high and cloudy, we do return to the larger patterns to cast a bigger shadow and cover more water, but our smaller prey-size flies remain more successful day in and day out.

TIGER MUSKIES

An Interview with Greg Pearson

Kip Vieth: Tell me about the difference between a tiger muskie and a natural muskie.

Greg Pearson: Apart from the physical appearance, I would say that a tiger is basically 90 percent natural and 10 percent pike. I have fished [tiger] muskies in the Midwest and they act very much like a natural. They are just as moody, and I know people that have chased both say that a tiger can sometimes be more muskie-like than a natural muskie.

KV: Tell me about your fishery and the differences between it and typical Midwest waters.

GP: The waters that have muskies are your typical western reservoirs. They are used for irrigation and other water needs. The water levels change as drawdown begins, and you have to be aware of that. An island may have 5 feet of water in the spring and then be 5 feet out of the water during the summer. Holding water varies a lot throughout the season. That island that is underwater during the spring offered excellent cover and holding water. During the summer we'll have to look at other cover, such as weed lines and breaks with a good transition area—typical muskie areas that you would find elsewhere throughout North America. Tigers don't reproduce, so we totally rely on stocking to supplement our fisheries. Tigers were first introduced here in Utah in 1989. They were stocked to help control the boom-and-bust cycle of panfish populations. The thinking was that the tigers would help control the populations and make for a steady and more reliable biomass in the reservoirs. We now have many quality fisheries throughout the West, and it has become a very fast-growing sport here. We now have a Muskies Inc. chapter here in Utah that continues to promote muskie opportunities and educate people about muskies and what a wonderful fish they are and how to properly handle them.

KV: What is your favorite time of year to fish for tigers?

GP: For fly fishing I like the early part of the season, from right after ice-off till when the water temperatures reach the mid-60s or so. I call this the finesse season. It is when the fly angler can really do their thing. It's the classic cat-and-mouse game. The trick is to see the fish following your fly as soon as possible. Western reservoirs are very clear, so you can see them coming from a fairly good distance. As soon as I see one, I automatically go into the tease mode. I try to manipulate the fly to trigger a response from the fish. The clear water lets you look at the fish and see what is getting it excited. It's a very visual game and a ton of fun. The muskies follow the bait, i.e., crappies and other panfish, into the shallows as they spawn. This makes the muskies easier to target, and you can often see them in the shallows. One advantage of the West is that an angler can follow the cool temps up in elevations. When it is mid-July and the dog days of summer on a reservoir, all one has to do is go to waters that are higher in elevation with cooler water temps and you'll find those finesse fish. The best temps for sight fishing seem to be in that 56- to 68-degree range.

KV: How big do the tigers get, and what's your personal best?

GP: My personal best is 47 inches and the state records is 49 inches, 33 pounds and 9 ounces. The catch-and-release record is 53¼ inches.

KV: Those are solid fish no matter where you're fishing. I always thought that tigers didn't get that big, but those are some large and impressive fish. I might have to make a trip out there to fish. What are the summer months like in the West? What we would call the dog days of summer here in the Midwest.

GP: The summer months are probably the hardest for the fly angler. Here in the West that is July till mid-September. As the water begins to warm, the fly is less effective and gear anglers begin to have the advantage. It's all about burning bucktails and other large baits for the most part. The fly angler is limited with that type of fishing. I call it Burn 1, 2, or 3. What we try to do is cover as much water as possible. I usually fish at a Burn 2 level, stripping fairly fast. When I see a muskie I then go into Burn 3, which is rod in the armpit, hand-over-hand stripping as fast as possible. I also switch to bigger flies. We start throwing stuff that you guys throw a lot of in the Midwest. Large flies that push a lot of water and cause a lot of disturbance. Like Eric [Grajewski] would use out on Lake St. Clair. It's a lot more work during those summer days and can be exhausting, and every retrieve needs to be finished with a figure eight or at least a J. No pain no gain, though.

KV: What are the fall months like? Here in the Upper Midwest, it is the best time to fish in my opinion.

GP: It can be good, but I still think the early summer period is the best for the fly angler. We just don't have that big fall push like you guys have. There is certainly very good fishing to be had, but I like the early summer the best for consistency. I think it also has a lot to do with the visual aspect of the fishing that time of year. The water is clear in the early part of the year, and seeing the fish and watching them eat your fly is as good as it gets.

KV: Do tigers react to moon phases and major and minor feeding times?

GP: I pay some attention to them, but I fish when I can. I'm only ten minutes from my home water, so when I get a chance to go, I go. Is there something to it? Absolutely. I think those bigger fish are affected by it more than the smaller ones. I have friends that trophy hunt and they pay very close attention to the lunar phases. I think that weather is the number one factor, but the lunar events certainly have a role in it. If I was chasing a state record or something, it would certainly be on my radar.

KV: Do you fish topwater at all?

GP: Yes, we fish it when we have the opportunity. It's all about water temperatures. I feel that 72 to 74 degrees is the optimum temp for topwater. The fish are active with the warmer water temps and they're willing to blow a topwater fly up. It's a ton of fun watching those big fish eat a topwater presentation.

KV: What is your hookup percentage? I know a lot of guys struggle with this when they are fishing topwater presentations.

GP: Actually, ours can be pretty good.

KV: Tell me your secret.

GP: I use a large Gurgler-type topwater fly. The hook is very exposed, it moves a lot of water, and there isn't that big foam head to try and rip through a muskie's teeth to get that hook into them. I use a 5/0 hook, so there is plenty of hook to get into their mouth.

KV: Just goes to show you never stop learning in this game. That's brilliant. That is why I've never been a big topwater fan, but you can rest assured that some of those will find their way into my fly box. I've never been a big fan of them for smallmouth fishing, but that does make sense for muskies. Now tell me about the future of tigers in the West. Does it look good?

GP: The future is pretty good, I think. A lot of anglers are discovering tiger muskies and what quality fisheries we have here in the western United States. The stocking program is strong for the most part. The reservoir that is my home water has a quota of 20,000. The states are recognizing the value of muskies to anglers and to biologists as a management tool. Groups like Muskies Inc. are now involved with the state agencies and doing some important work. They began a tagging program together in Utah three years ago, and some good information has already been gathered on growth rates. More data will be gathered over the years to come, and we will learn more and more about the biology of the tiger muskie here in the West. The future is exciting.

THE FRENCH RIVER AREA OF ONTARIO

An Interview with Andy Pappas

Andy Pappas has been the owner and main guide with Vicious Fishes Guide Service since 2007. He specializes in helping clients catch muskies in the French River area of Ontario, Canada. He also coordinates fishing-themed events for groups of various sizes, from family reunions to corporate retreats. Muskies Canada Inc., Canada's primary organization supporting research and conservation initiatives related to muskies, named Andy to its Hall of Fame in 2013. For more information about Andy's guiding and event coordination services, check out www.viciousfishes.ca.

Kip Vieth: I know very little about fishing Canada except for western Ontario and the Rainy Lake area where I fished as a kid with my family. I would imagine a lot of other people in the United States have very limited knowledge about Canada and muskie. Tell me about the area that you guide in.

Andy Pappas: I concentrate my guiding in the French River area of Ontario. For those not familiar with the area, we are about four and a half hours north of Toronto. Some of the waters that I fish are the Georgian Bay of Lake Huron, Lake Nipissing, and at least a dozen other lakes and systems in the area. It's a very overlooked area. It has everything a muskie angler could want. We have systems that are numbers lakes—by that I mean there are a good amount of fish in those waters. Then we have the larger bodies of waters that hold some truly remarkable fish. We're talking 50-inch class or above muskies. We are really blessed with some wonderful resources.

KV: Tell me about your fly-fishing experience and how you got started in it.

AP: I'm relatively new to it. I think it was five years ago when Colin McKeown of the television show *The New Fly Fisher* called me and was interested in filming a show with me. I had never fly-fished before. I said I would love to, and so the journey began. I knew I could put him on some fish but knew nothing about the fly game. I figured if I was going to do the show, I better learn about it and know how it worked and what I was getting myself into. I got a fly rod and started the process of learning how to fly-fish and pursue muskies with it. I guess the biggest things that I wanted to learn were what it's going to take to be successful and the limitations of the fly angler. It was something new and you can always learn in this game, and having another way to muskie fish is always a good thing. You can never have too many options when you're out chasing muskies.

KV: What are your thoughts on fly fishing for muskies since you started?

AP: It's opened another door for me, and I've really grown to like it. Ninety-nine percent of my guide trips are still done with conventional fishing gear. I think more conventional anglers should try fly fishing. It's like I said earlier, it gives you another way to approach muskie fishing. It teaches you a great deal. If you're learning something, it's just going to make you a better angler.

KV: Do you think that fly fishing is growing in Canada? I know that here in Minnesota, walleye is king and it would seem that Canada is the same way. I'd say that it's growing here, but it's a tough sell for those dyed-in-the-wool conventional anglers or the purist trout fly angler.

AP: To be honest, I'm not so sure. I can honestly say that I don't think that I've ever seen anyone on the water fly-fishing in the area that I guide in. It seems that it's just not something that most Canadians are looking to get into. We have a vast amount of water and maybe that is why, but I'm just not seeing many anglers gravitating toward fly fishing. Most of my fly angler clients are from the United States. You're a smallmouth guide, so you know how good smallmouth are on the fly. We aren't even getting people pursuing them on the fly. We have a ton of great fish to pursue

Big bugs often equal big fish.
ANDY PAPPAS

on the fly besides muskies. I would love to see the sport grow in this area. It really is an untapped resource for the fly angler in Canada. The water is so vast up here that the opportunities are almost endless. Fish just don't get conditioned, even by conventional anglers. Now, you throw a fly at them and it is really something different, and the fish's curiosity kicks in and it can really make a big difference. The fly can be a very effective way to catch muskies, especially in the early season.

KV: Tell me about the flies that you throw when you do chase them with the fly rod.

AP: Just like conventional gear, I like to ask the question, "What do I need to do to get those big fish to eat?" I'm a firm believer in big flies equal big fish. Bigger fish live in big water. That is pretty much true wherever you fish. Now, big fish eat bigger meals. Present them with a meal, not a snack. Will they eat a smaller fly? Sure they will. I just think that if a large muskie is going to expend the energy to eat, it wants a large meal. Now add the larger body of water, and you need to make your presence known. You need to separate your fly from all the other things swimming in that large body of water. The larger-profile flies do that. They move a lot of water and let a large muskie know that you're in the neighborhood. Muskies are for the most part visual eaters, but it never hurts to also work their lateral line. The more senses you activate on a muskie, the better. It seems to me that those larger fish just like larger profiles.

I'd like to also say something about the size of hooks on a lot of the flies that I see out there. I just don't think that a lot of muskie flies are tied on the proper hooks. I like a large-gapped hook. I want to have the hook exposed so that I can drive that hook into a muskie's hard jaw as easily as possible. On a lot of the flies that I've seen over the years, the hooks just don't seem big enough. We have some excellent fly tiers here in Canada that make beautiful muskie flies and use super hooks to get the job done.

KV: If someone wanted to come up and chase muskies, what in your opinion is the best time of the year?

AP: The season starts the first weekend of June. I'd say from opener to early July is the best time to pursue muskies on the fly. The fish are for the most part in shallower water and are much easier to target with the fly rod. That is the one limiting factor with the fly rod, and that is depth and being able to cover a lot of water. In the early part of the season, the muskies are in the shallow water and a bit more concentrated. This makes for the opportune time to pursue them with a fly. Fishing is generally good all year. Muskies, as you know, can be easy to pattern throughout the year—it's just that early in the season, they are a bit easier to approach with the fly rod.

KV: Sounds like you have a hell of a fishery.

AP: Yes, we do. I'm just blessed to have such great resources. Like I said earlier, this area is vast and very overlooked by the fly angler. We have something for everyone. It can be smallmouth, pike, walleye, or, of course, muskie. Whatever your goal is, we stand a pretty good chance of helping you reach it here. We can target your first muskie or a trophy. It all depends what kind of experience you're looking for.

OTTAWA RIVER MUSKIE FACTORY

An Interview with John Anderson

John is a diversely experienced veteran of the musky world. He began guiding on the LOTW system over forty years ago and is the owner of the ottawarivermuskyfactory.com. Guide, author, researcher (saveamillionfish.com), educator, lure maker (muskyfactorybaits.com), and TV personality—John lives muskies 365 days a year and loves it. He has also been a proud member of Muskies Canada for over twenty-five years and represents them publicly at shows and events throughout North America.

Kip Vieth: Tell me about you and the guide program that you are running.

John Anderson: Well, I've been guiding since the mid-seventies. I guided for many species, but muskies are what have really grabbed me. I have a passion for them, and the more I learn about them, the more they intrigue me. I guide about 170 days a year for them right know. I really love being involved with their conservation and the research that is being done right now. I'm very involved with Muskies Canada. Similar to Muskies Inc. in the States, they are a great organization that is educating people on just how special a large muskie is and how they need to be protected. Research that is taking place now by our natural resource professionals is groundbreaking. The more we learn about these amazing fish, the more we can protect them and ensure a bright future for the muskie. The research is really fascinating.

KV: How many of those 170 trips are fly-fishing trips?

JA: I do about twenty trips or so a year that are fly anglers.

KV: Tell me about your home water.

JA: I do most of my guiding on the Ottawa River. It is 900 miles long. Muskies can be found in about 200 miles of the river. It is the biggest tributary of the St. Lawrence. It is over 300 feet deep in spots, and there are plenty of spots where it is 100 feet deep. It's a deep and large river system. I do most of my guiding in between the cities of Ottawa and Montreal.

KV: If I wanted to come up by you and chase muskies on the fly, what in your opinion is the best time of the year?

JA: I think that the first two weeks in July are prime time. The fish have spawned and have recuperated and are moving into their summer haunts. This time of the year is the beginning of the summer season, and they seem just a little bit more willing to eat. They haven't been educated yet and so they seem to be a little more cooperative. It's kind of the equivalent of our first trip of the summer to the beach or lake. We know that summer has arrived and are super excited to be in our summer happy places. The muskies are glad to have arrived at their summer homes and looking to eat and get comfortable. Now that is all weather dependent, but it is usually the beginning of July when it happens.

KV: Tell me about your forage base on the Ottawa.

JA: The biggest forage base that the muskies take advantage of is the mooneye. There is a very good population, and they are your typical muskie meal—a softer fish and plenty of fatty flesh that muskies seem to key on. They know what puts on the pounds and that is the forage that they seem to be drawn to.

KV: That's the truth—they love those big fatty meals. In our area they key up suckers and tullibees.

JA: They love that type of meal. That brings me to a point I want to make: Big muskies just don't eat that often. They eat a big meal and then rest and digest it. They spend about two-thirds of their time just lying on the bottom in an inactive state. If you just think about that and do the math, this makes them even more difficult to catch. It's hard to catch them when they don't eat. Add their low-density numbers and the fact that you're fishing them with a fly rod, and it can seem like a pretty daunting task.

KV: You make it sound almost impossible to get the job done with a fly rod. What would you say are a few keys to success with the fly rod then?

JA: There are a few things that I would tell the fly angler to keep in mind. The first is that there are always fish on weeds. No matter what, it seems like they're just a natural draw to the fish and there are always a few holding on them. If ever in doubt, work the weeds.

The other thing I would say is to look for the bait. Depending on the time of the year, the fly can be very effective. In the fall the emerald shiners in our system school up. With the shiners come other fish, including muskies. Working the emerald shiner schools can really pay off. Working to these baitfish with a slower fly can often bring up a muskie that is keyed up on wounded bait. A big fly that moves water and looks like something wounded is often the trigger that is needed. Using their lateral line to locate bait is often overlooked by the fly angler. A fly that moves water and causes an underwater disturbance can play an important role in a muskie tracking down your fly. Sometimes that slower movement of the fly can make a difference. There have been studies done that have shown how important the lateral line is to a muskie's tracking down its next meal. They use it and the angler should take advantage of it if possible.

KV: Pressure seems to be playing a bigger and bigger role in our fishing here in the Upper Midwest and most likely throughout the country. How is the pressure in your system, and do you think that it plays a role in a fly angler's success?

JA: It isn't that big of an issue for us here in Canada at this time, but I can understand your question. I have seen it play a bigger role as the years go by. I have seen it especially when I was participating in muskie tournaments on more-pressured water. On my water I think if a large muskie is caught that it remembers the experience and learns pretty quickly what caused a very bad experience. I continually move my spots and fish a lot of unpressured water. I keep moving from the spots that I have caught fish or have pressured over a period of time. Once I've caught a large muskie, I just figure that fish isn't going to be caught again that year. I move on and look for other water with a less-educated fish.

Another thing that I'm seeing, and other professionals too, is that more muskies are getting caught boatside than ever before. I would say that today 50 percent of the fish that I land are caught at the boat. Not too long ago that number was probably more like 20 percent. The fish just seem more cautious these days just because they are learning the hard way. You really need to have your boatside A game. I see it a lot, when anglers just don't have a real good close-quarters game. It's important to practice and remain calm. I believe in doing just a simple oval rather than a figure eight. Less can go wrong with just a simple oval, and I also believe in changing depths while you're turning the oval.

Reading the fish and getting them to eat comes with practice. More time on the water is the only thing that can give you that experience. My final word of advice is just to spend time on the water and the pieces of the puzzle will start to come together. I will say, however, that the puzzle is never really put together all the way.

INDEX

Italicized page numbers indicate illustrations. Tables are indicated with "t" following the page number.